Stay Tuned

My Life
Behind the Mic

By Bill Diehl

For Lorry, Suzanne, Doug, Teddy, and Lyla

Contents

Foreword

OK, I'll admit it: I never heard, or heard of, Bill Diehl until I met him at ABC Radio News.

It was April 1974 when I was first hired as a "vacation-relief" news writer at ABC. And there was Bill Diehl, the morning drive-time anchor of ABC's Entertainment Network, preparing his newscasts with nervous energy: scanning wire copy; reading verbatim transcripts of taped correspondent reports or news "actualities," ABC's word for sound bites; typing away onto color-coded multi-carbon sets; handing his copy to an editor to be checked for accuracy; then off to the air studio, often with his shirt-tail flying out of his pants, before sitting down in Studio 5, putting on his headphones, and delivering his newscast in the strong, clear, warm voice that belonged to Bill Diehl.

It turns out Bill and I have some things in common besides our first names. Bill was on the radio in his small town in upstate New York while in high school; I was known as "The Voice" of my high school public address system. Bill is a proud graduate of Ithaca College and its Radio-TV school; several years later, I went to Ithaca as a Radio-TV major but transferred out after my freshman year. Bill learned his craft at low-paying broadcast jobs before he got his shot at WNEW; I too worked for a pittance at small stations before I got a break and a chance to work, part time, at WNEW. But Bill had already gone to ABC a few years earlier.

The ABC radio newsroom back then was a boy's club with very few women on the air, at the editor's desk, or in management. That changed of course as the 1970s closed in on the 1980s, but there was definitely a "male" atmosphere to the room when I first got there with a gang of guys who kept up a constant chatter of jokes and insults. Sometimes, to his dismay, Bill became the target of their foolishness.

But Bill Diehl was a hard worker, pounding out newscasts on large-type Olympia typewriters, calling to set up interviews with celebrities, rushing off to this event or the other. Eventually, as this book reveals, Bill's work shifted away from the hour-to-hour, day-to-day news, to covering only entertainment and celebrities. As good a radio newsperson as Bill was, he was even better covering show-biz, which he did enthusiastically and joyfully.

Someone at ABC Radio News had early on given Bill the sobriquet of "Mr. Media," and the name stuck because it so accurately described Bill's complete dedication to the job of covering entertainment.

After a while, Bill got his own office away from the newsroom, an office filled all around with books, CDs, videos, and especially the tapes of all the people he had interviewed, ready to be used in his daily show-biz program, or longer weekend pieces, or obituaries. To say that Bill Diehl knows where the bodies are buried—or more accurately— where the dead celebrities' sound bites are, is a compliment to his many years of interviews of the famous, soon-to-be famous, and formerly famous. Even after his "retirement" as a full-time ABC News radio correspondent, Bill continues to return frequently to the newsroom, offering features on a celebrity's new book, big birthday, or their passing. He's a welcome and beloved person; the last man standing from the glory days of ABC Radio News going back almost 50 years; a friend and mentor to many who work there now, or who've moved on to different places or bigger jobs.

I'm glad to call Bill Diehl a friend and I enjoyed learning more about his life in this book, and "listening" to his take on some of the well-known people he got a chance to interview over his more than 45 years—and counting—at ABC Radio News.

Mr. Media, indeed.

Bill Stoller
A news writer, editor
and on-air correspondent at
ABC Radio News

Preface

The idea for this memoir grew out of a March 2014 article I wrote for the *Silurian News* called "My Life in Show Business." The Silurians, founded in 1924, is the oldest journalist society in America. The article was clearly grist for a book that triggered an expanded journey into not just a "life in show business," but a career that contained many facets of my love for radio and some TV too.

I began my career in broadcasting a long time ago, stretching back more than half a century. It started as a bit of a lark; call it "radio make believe." My parents probably thought it was nice that their son was "playing radio". But I loved it so much it became my passion, which continues to this day. I owe them a lot, they never interfered.

People in this radio business tend to float around a lot but I have been truly fortunate, working for only five radio stations during my entire career and one network, ABC.

This journey has afforded me the opportunity to meet and interview some of the biggest names in news and entertainment. It doesn't get any better than that.

Acknowledgments

How do I thank so many wonderful people? Until now, I had never written a book. Yes, over a long career I had written and voiced many newscasts, show biz feature stories, and even obituaries. But this memoir, *Stay Tuned: My Life Behind the Mic*, has been new territory. So here goes.

First, a big thank you to Barbara Lovenheim, author and close friend, who suggested I contact Emily at Bookmasters of Ashland, Ohio. Emily is Emily McQuate, and she and her team with Sharon Anderson have worked closely with me from beginning to end.

Besides Bookmasters, I have been fortunate to have several editors along the way, beginning with Deborah Harkins, a former editor (26 years) at *New York* magazine. Debbie read an early rough draft, cleaned it up, and made it presentable. Bill Stoller, who wrote a terrific foreword, has been invaluable in tackling an often disjointed manuscript and making it so much better, especially tapping into his ABC News history, so very important. Several others received advance copies of the manuscript including author Linda Erin Keenan, who offered advice, especially on the look of the book's cover.

I would be terribly remiss if I did not thank my colleagues at ABC News Radio. Among them, news vice president Steve Jones and his support staff, Andrew Kalb, Wayne Fisk, Heidi Oringer, Larry Lafferty, Ryan Kessler, Jeff Fitzgerald, Kevin Rider, Greg Laub, and Irma Aviles. We have the best editors in the business. One of them is Andrea Dresdale, manager, entertainment programming, who does a great job editing my obituary pieces. Thank you Andrea. Kudos to David Blaustein, my successor who has done a stellar job as chief entertainment correspondent. David also took the photo for the book's back cover, and Sarah Sweeney, you gave it a final touch-up.

Mary Lou Grisell Krol, it was a pleasure working with you in the studio in earlier years and when we traveled to L.A. for the Academy Awards. Dave Alpert, you were there too. We were a good team putting together our live and taped backstage reports. And in New York, thanks to ABC's Chuck Sivertsen who anchored and edited our live Oscar packages. Maureen Gillespie of SmartPR, you have been in my corner from the beginning with your expert advice and counsel.

My parents, William Bernard and Signe Youngstrom Diehl, deserve special mention for their support. I'm glad they lived to see their son carve out a successful career on network radio and even saw him on TV too.

Lastly, a huge thanks to my wonderful wife Lorry, who has put up with my penchant for flea markets, filling drawers, closets, and a bookcase full of huge amounts of broadcasting memorabilia. Although she is a very successful author, she mostly kept hands off this memoir, believing it was a story I should tell myself without much interference.

My life has been a delightful journey. Who knows what lies ahead? "Stay Tuned," or borrowing a line from Charles Osgood, "I'll see you on the radio!"

Part I

The Making of a Network Newscaster

Chapter 1

A Crystal-Set Kid

I can hear it even now, more than 60 years later. My dad and I were strolling past radio station WCLI in Corning, New York. The station was owned by our local newspaper, *The Evening Leader*. I could see the station's control room, up some stairs from the street. It was a hot summer day and the door was open. A man was standing near the control board, and I could clearly hear the program being broadcast— *The Lone Ranger!* From the top of the stairs came the dramatic voice of announcer Fred Foy, delivering the legendary opening: "Return with us now to those thrilling days of yesteryear. A fiery horse with the speed of light, a cloud of dust, and a hearty Hi-Yo Silver! The Lone Ranger rides again!" Little did this 10-year-old boy know, back then, that many years later he would become a correspondent at ABC and Fred Foy would be introducing him on the radio.

It was clear, early on, that radio would be in my blood. When I was 10 or 11 I built a crystal set at home. I would take a small wire, known as a cat whisker, mounted on a board, and touch it to different areas on the crystal, and

Announcer Fred Foy, the man with the compelling voice.

suddenly a radio station could be heard on my headset. This may not sound like much these days, but back then I found it quite exciting.

I was really hooked when I bought a wireless microphone from Allied Radio in Chicago. It allowed me to choose a frequency and broadcast to a radio in our kitchen. But having an audience of just my parents wasn't enough.

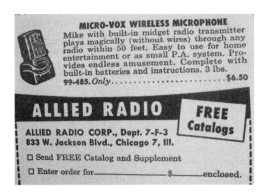

MICRO-VOX WIRELESS MICROPHONE
Mike with built-in midget radio transmitter plays magically (without wires) through any radio within 50 feet. Easy to use for home entertainment or as small P.A. system. Provides endless amusement. Complete with built-in batteries and instructions. 3 lbs.
99-485. *Only* $6.50

ALLIED RADIO   FREE Catalogs

ALLIED RADIO CORP., Dept. 7-F-3
833 W. Jackson Blvd., Chicago 7, Ill.

☐ Send FREE Catalog and Supplement
☐ Enter order for_____$_____enclosed.

If I attached the little antenna on the wireless mic to a long antenna that stretched between our house and the garage, I could broadcast for several blocks in my neighborhood. I set up a little studio in the basement and read stories from the newspaper and played music too. I even distributed a program schedule to neighbors and put up a sign atop the garage using the call letters WABD (William Andrew Billy Diehl). With my microphone picking up music on a radio in my little makeshift studio, I would ride around the neighborhood on my bicycle with a transistor radio to see how far my little signal would travel. Once a town bus went by our house and I remember taking my microphone on a "remote broadcast," interviewing the bus driver when he made his stop at our corner.

One day a neighbor across the street, Paul Yorio, who was a ham radio operator, knocked on our door. My father answered, and Yorio asked, "Is someone operating a radio station at your house? You know that's illegal, and the Federal Communications Commission could come to your house and have you and your son arrested." My dad hastily headed to my little basement studio and said, "Shut this thing down; we could be in trouble with the FCC!"

My father need not have worried, because very soon I would be on the air with a real radio station, in Corning. It was WCLI, which had now moved to brand new studios in its own building. My dad was there with me one day and here we are, with me sitting at the station's control board.

On Saturday mornings, the station broadcast a show called *Youth Bureau Time*, and I was chosen to be the announcer for the program.

One day, after our program ended the station manager, George Droelle, said, "Hey, kid, you've got a pretty good voice—how would you like to work for us?" I couldn't believe it. I was going to be broadcasting at a real radio station! I got a Third Class Radio Telephone license (I had to take a test), necessary to turn the transmitter on and off and take meter readings each hour, as required by the FCC. I made my on-air debut in December of 1955, at 15. Droelle was a great motivator in my career, telling me, "Once you get radio in your blood, it will always be with you."

He was so right!

Droelle was also WCLI's sports director. The station broadcast the Corning Red Sox games—home and away. For the away games, Droelle and News Director Dick Tobias (he loved sports) would sit in the studio next to a

The author with his father at the WCLI control board.

Western Union teletype operator, who would be getting on a ticker tape a play-by-play rundown. We had crowd noise we had recorded from our stadium in Corning, and it would play on tape while Droelle and Tobias announced the game. They would read it off the ticker tape—*ball one, strike one, home run*—and make it sound quite real. They had two pieces of wood that they would clap for a big hit. I ran the control board, raising the volume on the crowd tape for a big hit for the hometown team, which was part of the Class D Pony League.

Bill, the announcer, on Youth Bureau Time.

I worked Saturdays at WCLI, running the control board all by myself; I even had my own program, *The Bill Diehl Show*, from 10 to midnight. I was a real disc jockey, spinning records. By my senior year in high school I was filling in for full-time staffers (including the morning man) when they went on vacation. We had a couple of tape recorders in the control room, and I recorded one of my Saturday night shows. Somehow the reel-to-reel tape survived, and I still have it, from the spring of 1958. My theme music was "The Midnight Blues," by the Nelson Riddle orchestra. The rest of my playlist that night included "Speak Low," Ray Conniff; "Return to Me," Dean Martin; "I've Got Bells on My Heart," Jane Morgan; "Too Close for Comfort," Johnny Mathis; "Romance Me," the DeMarco sisters; "I Didn't Know What Time It Was," Frank Sinatra; "Say You're Mine," Lillian Brooks from the movie *Peyton Place*, which later became a popular TV series. I wrapped up that night with "That's All," by Tommy Edwards. I sounded young, but there I was, a teenager, on the radio in my hometown.

But what were my hopes down the line? To become a big-city DJ? Maybe an announcer? At times I had visions of announcing on a network like NBC, saying, "The following program is brought to you in living color on NBC." One of WCLI's DJs was Bob Shaddock, who became an icon in the market. The station was founded by *The Corning Leader*, and until WCLI was sold and moved, the radio studios were in the newspaper building, next to the Erie Railroad tracks. Passing trains shook the whole building, including the turntables as they played 78 rpm records. The late *Leader* columnist Dick Peer remembered Shaddock picking up the arm on the turntable, making announcements until the train passed, and then dropping the needle back down at the same spot so the song being played would continue and listeners wouldn't miss a beat. Nice little trick.

Chapter 2

"Local Radio at Its Craziest"

Graduation came at Corning's Northside High. Next stop, Ithaca College, where I enrolled in the school's Radio-TV department. Radio, by the way, still came first in the fall of 1958. It was more than a dozen years more before television got top billing.

Ithaca College's then new communications center was located above the school's library. For its time it was quite a modern facility, housing both the college radio station, WICB-FM, and television studios too. (There was also an AM station, but it was "carrier-current" to only the college's dorms.) Students not only could work on WICB radio but also on WICB-TV, which had a link to the town's cable system and for a few hours each evening we were on the air doing a variety of programs, news, interviews, and a program called *Showcase*. I did some news and was also the announcer for a few programs.

9

The author on Ithaca College's TV station.

Besides courses in broadcasting I also took required courses in biology, history, and political science. I quickly realized that college broadcasting did not satisfy my appetite for expanding a career that had begun in Corning. So I got a job at a local commercial radio station in Ithaca, WTKO. The station was known for hiring students, especially those from Ithaca College. Soon I was on the air, doing news, and on weekends a DJ stint. World and national news came from ABC Radio but I read local news. Phone calls to the city police, sheriff's office and fire department gave me reports on any accidents or fires. I would type up a script and also steal stories from newspapers, *The Ithaca Journal*, *Syracuse Post Standard* (which had an Ithaca section), and even the *Cornell Daily Sun*. Often when I didn't have time to rewrite newspaper stories I would ad-lib around them. Don't think I even attributed stories to the papers unless it was an exclusive. It was truly what we called "rip and read."

We had one wire service, the Associated Press. There were newscasters on TV and radio who I admired. For a time, I even started sounding a bit like David Brinkley, but I grew out of it when I went to Washington. If I did a newscast I was usually in a separate studio and the DJ was at the controls and played any commercials within my 'cast.

In a couple of years, the station's news director left and I became the station's news chief. Pretty heady stuff, writing and reading news — even doing editorials on local issues in the community. The station, an ABC Radio affiliate, was competing with a very staid, rather old-world station, WHCU, which carried CBS programming. TKO, as our station was dubbed, played pop music; as the "new kids on the block" we were looked down upon by those staffers at WHCU. But we were enterprising, with a station manager who would try anything to get listener attention. The station bought a little car with three wheels, an Isetta. The call letters were painted on the side of it and it became WTKO Mobile Unit Number 1. There was, of course no Number 2. We didn't cover any news stories with it, but it was good for publicity.

Trade deals were a way of life back then at many small-town radio stations. We constantly aired commercials for a local supermarket called Atwater's; some ran as long as two minutes. Most were 30 seconds or a minute. We had no proof, but rumor had it that the station owner got free food from the store.

Once we had a treasure-hunt contest, hiding something somewhere in town, with a cash prize for the person who found the "treasure." We also had a fire radio installed in the newsroom, and one day I was told that we were starting something new. When we heard a fire call I was told to interrupt programming and tell listeners about the fire that had just broken out in the Ithaca area. Here's how our slogan went: "When the fire bell rings and the siren wails, tune to TKO for all the details." At the end of the fire report, I was to say, "This fire report has been brought to you by the McKinney Insurance Agency of Ithaca. Remember, for all your insurance needs, it's McKinney."

Our fire reports didn't go on very long. The fire chief called the station to complain that we couldn't do this — we were causing traffic problems, since some listeners in their cars raced to the scene of the fire. Said the chief, "They're getting there before our trucks arrive, and it's dangerous." Ah yes, that was local radio at its craziest.

A local police officer became a big fan of the station, so much so that he learned how to get the station up and running in the morning. (We were a "day-timer" so under FCC rules we had to leave the air at sunset). The cop was given a key, and he would turn on the transmitter, put a long-playing album on the turntable, then, in his patrol car, pick up the morning man at his house and deliver him to the studio. At Christmastime, one of our DJs read letters to Santa, and since we had no echo chamber the TKO Santa put a wastebasket on his head while reading them.

While all this was going on, I was still taking classes at Ithaca College, sandwiching in courses while working at the station. I did a morning newscast, raced to the college for a class, returned to do a noon newscast. Occasionally I also played DJ. We had a show from Fred's Record Shop, about a block from the station. I would do my newscast, and while a five-minute weather show was on the air following my newscast, I would run down the street a couple of blocks to Fred's, where we had a little turntable and a microphone in the window. A clerk at the store, Betty Shufelt (hard to forget a name like that), would have a record or album the store was promoting ready to play and off we'd go, a live show from the store. Drivers would let us know they were listening by honking their horns as they passed by.

After the show I was off to another class at the college and then back to the radio station to record an editorial for the next day. Sometimes I would be at the college in the evening, doing a show on WICB-TV. Looking back at it now, I don't know how I did it all. I did not live on campus; I lived with several roommates at two different locations, one of them above Big Jim's Pizza. It was close to the station and I could go across the street in the early morning to do my newscast by climbing up the fire escape in the back and coming in through the control room window.

Below is a photo of me at the WTKO control board, spinning records. Sorry the quality isn't better, but you can see three tape recorders in the back of the control room. The last one did not have a remote start on the control board. Luckily, our chair had wheels, so if I had to play back a commercial on the third tape machine I would turn off the mic and roll the chair back to the window and quickly

turn the tape recorder on. It could all be accomplished in less than 5 seconds.

I was never cut out to be a DJ, although my friend Tommy Saunders, who worked briefly at TKO, was the real deal, with lines like "I'm making the scene with my record machine and my little flat friends the records. Time to go, I'll pick up my stacks of wax and hit the tracks." Tommy went on to WOLF in Syracuse, then to WKBW, Buffalo, and finally to KYA and KOIT, both in San Francisco, before he retired a few years ago.

Wedding bells rang for me in '63. I married an Ithaca College student, Dianne Sears, in June.

Later that year, the country was shaken, when on November 22 President John F. Kennedy was assassinated. I was having lunch at our apartment when a soap opera was interrupted with a bulletin: Walter Cronkite, of CBS, breaking the news we didn't want to hear—that JFK did not survive and had died at Parkland Hospital in Dallas. I was news director of WTKO then. I rushed back to the station, grabbed a small tape recorder, and went out on the streets of Ithaca to get reaction to what had happened. TKO was an ABC affiliate, so we went with the network's feed. Correspondent Don Gardiner was the anchor. (In the 1970s, when I became a correspondent at ABC, I worked with Gardiner. I should also note that at ABC I met Cronkite several times—once on the ferryboat heading to Martha's Vineyard, where Cronkite had a home, and once in our studio to talk about his amazing career.)

When my bride graduated in 1964, we were off to Washington, D.C.—she to get a master's degree in social work at Catholic University, and me to hunt for work.

Chapter 3

Moving Up to 50,000 Watts

I arrived in Washington in May, 1964. I had left WTKO making the princely sum of $125 a week. I earned extra cash, 50 bucks, announcing the stock-car races at the Ithaca Dryden Speedway. Luckily I soon got a job in D.C., as a writer for Maury Povich (the same Povich who now hosts a popular syndicated TV show) on radio station WWDC. It was $90 a week, but hey, I needed a job; I had a wife to support. But fate soon played a wonderful hand. My college friend and roommate in his last semester, Chet Curtis, who was now a reporter working at the CBS-TV station in Washington, WTOP, called me and said there was an opening for a morning newscaster on WTOP radio. I auditioned and got the job. In less than 10 years I had earned a spot working at a 50,000-watt powerhouse station in the nation's capital. How cool is that?

The author in the TOP newsroom.

Management liked me enough to expand my radio duties and gave me a five-minute TV newscast, *The Mid-Morning News with Bill Diehl.* We had recently installed our first Ampex Video tape machine (two-inch videotape) and an engineer kindly taped my first newscast, January 3, 1966. I was only 24, looked young on TV, but I got through it without any mistakes.

(If you're curious, it's now on YouTube, https://youtu.be/ktqYs_vUC_M)

My TV newscast followed a kids' show, *Ranger Hal.* Once (wish I had a tape of this) during my telecast a young girl got lost in the studio as the other kids were leaving. She came up to me on my platform and interrupted me to ask, "Mister, what are you doing?" Flustered at first, I looked around for the floor director, whom I couldn't find, so I told the youngster, "Young lady I'm trying to do a newscast, and if you'll leave, I'll finish it." About then the floor director woke up and hustled the girl out of the studio.

I should mention that besides Chet (my wife and I became godparents to one of his children, Dawn), the station's staff included Sam Donaldson, who became nationally famous when he was hired as a correspondent at ABC News, based in Washington. Sam was quite a character — very bright, but also full of himself. Once, when something went wrong on his TV newscast at WTOP Sam returned to the newsroom, jumped atop a desk, and shouted, "I'm surrounded by incompetence!"

Also at 'TOP were Max Robinson, who became a network correspondent on ABC; Bob Windsor, Hal Walker, and Bill Zimmerman, all of whom also went to ABC; and Warner ("Let's go to the videotape") Wolf, who later went to New York, working for both WABC-TV, and WCBS-TV. Warner is now part of the Don Imus morning team on radio and Fox TV.

Most of my work at WTOP was on the radio side. The staff was highly unionized — engineers wouldn't even let me move a microphone. I couldn't even do a station break — that was the job of a staff announcer. Being on-air meant I had to join AFTRA, the TV & radio performers' union, later merged with SAG, the movie actors' union.

On the overnight shift, 'TOP carried *Music 'Til Dawn*, sponsored by American Airlines. It was also heard, with separate announcers, on nine other stations across the country. I anchored the 11 p.m. news, *The World Tonight. One* night when I finished the broadcast the host of *Music 'Til Dawn*, Terry Hourigan, had not shown up. I looked at the engineer, and he pointed to me. So that beautiful *MTD* theme, a variation on "That's All," by Sy Mann, began playing, and I got to say "American Airlines greets you with *Music 'Til Dawn.*" While the theme was still playing, a breathless Hourigan walked into the studio and said, "Nice job, Bill, but better stick to news."

WTOP was located in what was called the Broadcast House, a beautiful, modern state-of-the art facility with both radio and television studios. In the lobby were big photos of the station's air personalities. One day one of them was walking in and a maintenance man was taking down his photo. "What are you doing?" he asked. "I don't know," he said. "I was just told to take it down." A short time later, the announcer confronted his boss, who apologized, saying that a memo was going out but somehow mistakenly went out too early. One of my 'TOP colleagues used to pre-record his 8 p.m. newscast so he could have dinner with his ladylove and then return to do his 11 p.m. newscast. One night, however, either the tape playback was garbled or broke and the result was dead air. He got the axe. Luckily in my entire career in broadcasting I was never fired.

It was now late 1966, and with my marriage falling apart, fate again played another good hand. And once again my benefactor was an Ithaca College alum—Bernie Ruttenberg, who was doing publicity at WNEW radio in New York, one of the great independent stations in the nation. Bernie told me there was a part-time job open for a newscaster but it could become full-time, since several others might be leaving soon. One of them was Steve Bell, who was going to ABC Radio News. It wasn't long before Bell landed a job on television as the news reader on ABC's new morning program, then called *AM America*.

I got the job at WNEW. It was on a cold January in 1967 that I started on the overnight shift. Not very glamorous, but I couldn't be happier, I was on the air in the biggest market in the country. What an exciting place to work! Even the location was exciting, 565 Fifth Avenue.

WNEW was famous for its great air personalities— Klavan and Finch (the morning team), William B. Williams and his *Make-Believe Ballroom*, Pete Myers, Ted Brown, Jim Lowe. And it could boast a first-rate news department of more than 30 people, unheard of for an independent station at that time.

After only a few months at WNEW, I became a full-time staff newscaster. Alan Walden, who was news director at the time, said in a December 1967 memo, under the heading *Procedure*, "If you can keep your head when all around you are losing theirs, you obviously belong to the WNEW news department."

Being a part of this great station was a joy I'll never forget. The DJs—oops, it's a term management did not like; at WNEW they were air personalities—I got such a kick out of working with all of them, especially Gene Klavan and Dee Finch, Klavan gave me a copy of his 1964 book *We Die at Dawn.* He autographed it, saying, "To Bill, whose devotion and great talent have made him one of them."

The hijinks of Klavan and Finch were legendary. Once Klavan found a can of green paint that the city's Department of Traffic used to paint the green line on Fifth Avenue for the St. Patrick's Day Parade, which passed by the WNEW studios. Klavan painted a detour on the line—through WNEW's lobby, up the carpeted stairs to the second floor, where the station's studios were located.

WNEW billboard along the West Side Highway promoting the stations morning team.

WNEW played music from "The Great American Songbook," and some of the most talented singers often stopped by. On one of my first overnights, Steve Lawrence and Eydie Gorme showed up in the newsroom, and asked me for directions to the studio for an interview. On another night Tony Bennett appeared. Perhaps it was these celebrity drop-ins that excited me about the world of showbiz and later would lead me into that hallowed arena at ABC. Later I was able to interview Bennett for my program. (In Part II I've spotlighted my interviews with authors, film and Broadway stars, singers, sports figures, talk-show hosts, and other luminaries.)

Meanwhile at WNEW, Dick Shepard, host of the overnight show, *Milkman's Matinee*, had fun promoting my single status (I was newly divorced), calling me "New York's most eligible bachelor." Our 50,000-watt signal reached up and down the eastern seaboard. One day, a letter arrived from a woman in Maine. It included a photo with her mother and a child. The letter read, "If you'll pay for my plane fare I'll come to New York and we can get together." Needless to say, I was amused, but never took her up on it. In 1968, however, I met Lorraine (Lorry) Buscaglia, the woman I would marry the following year. Announcer Dennis Owen introduced us. Lorry was living in New York and working at Dramatist Play Service. My good friend Mike Eisgrau, who had joined WNEW as a reporter, was best man at our wedding. Lorry and I even teamed up at the station for a documentary dealing with endangered animals. *Where Have All the Animals Gone* won an Ohio State award. Reporter Chris Glenn helped edit and produce the program. Glenn and another 'NEW reporter, Steve Young, went to CBS News where both did some TV as well as radio.

WNEW became something like a farm team for the networks. When NBC started NIS, the short-lived News and Information Service, its 24-hour all-news program, WNEW's News Director Alan Walden joined NIS along with newscaster Edward Brown.

Chapter 4

Learning Not to
Be Too Clever

WNEW was an amazing station; there has never been one quite like it. I still have copies of memos from the station's news directors, who included Lee Hanna (who went to CBS), Alan Walden, and Mike Stein. Those memos were known simply as "Notes and Comments on Recent Newscasts." We all strived to get a good comment in the "Lines I Liked" column. Once, early on at WNEW, I tried too hard to be clever. On a 4 a.m. 'cast I wrote, "Another Viet Cong attack may be just around the pagoda." News director Walden heard it in his car, heading into the studio. He wasn't happy. "Another line like that, Diehl," he said, "and it's back to Washington." Lesson learned: *In the future, don't try to go overboard with cleverness.*

Vietnam came up again in one of my newscasts, but in a much different way. While I was reading a story about enemy casualties in Vietnam, I suddenly heard in my headphones Ted Brown saying, "Who turned the fucking lights off?" Brown had entered the air studio to start his show after my newscast, but somehow his mic had been left on. To make matters worse, I had paused in between stories just at the moment he blurted out the obscenity. It went by so fast that there were no complaints.

Another story from my time on the overnight was the "gorilla gag." I don't remember this happening, but John Venable, a desk assistant, says he was the culprit and the gag was played on me while I was doing a newscast on the *Milkman's Matinee*. Venable says, "I had typed up a story on AP carbons on a machine with a similar font to the news wires. I went running into the studio waving the copy; I handed it to Bill and he started to read, 'This just in: a large black gorilla has been sighted climbing. . .'" Venable says there was laughter on the air. He took some heat for his little stunt and was called on the carpet by News Director Mike Stein and the program director. He got a stern warning. Interesting that neither I nor Stein could recall this incident, but Venable says it did happen.

"And then there's Jane Fonda." That was the headline in a WNEW News brochure. Fonda was making a film called *Klute*, playing Bree Daniel, a New York City call girl. In the movie Bree awakens to the sound of a newscast on her clock radio. The station is WNEW. The newscaster is Jim Donnelly, but it was supposed to be ME. My shift had been changed, and so I missed my big chance to be in a Fonda film.

(I did get to meet Jane Fonda, several times when I became a correspondent at ABC Radio. My interviews with Fonda are in Part II of this book.)

A lot could be learned from the WNEW news director memos. I have a few from before I joined the 'NEW news staff.

A 1961 memo from Lee Hanna under the heading Yellow Newscasts: "Nikita Khrushchev, the Russian bear, warned the West." Said Hanna, "we're becoming increasingly editorial in writing about Khrushchev and Castro. References to the 'Russian bear' color our newscasts to an extent that is almost tabloid. Although I admit there is a strong temptation to take a verbal potshot at the Communist camp, I urge you to resist the temptation and play it straight."

Another from Hanna in '61: "Roosevelt Hospital. Rock 'n' Roll singer Jackie Wilson is in critical condition tonight after a woman admirer shot him six times at his apartment." Wrote Hanna: "If she had admired him any more she might have killed him."

- From News Director Alan Walden, May, 1968: "Erin Go Bragh! On one newscast I heard that millions of 'Gaelic' workers might be going back to their jobs in France. I assumed that either France had been invaded by Ireland, or the offending newscaster had mispronounced 'Gallic.'"

- Another from Walden: November, 1968. "If the RCA Victor dog had been required to listen to all the talks since the beginning of the school crisis, his ears would be worn to a frazzle." Said Walden, "Very cute. The lead should however have been preceded by the phrase. . . 'apropos of nothing' . . . cut it out."

- But Walden often found writing that sparkled, like this line on a police slowdown: "The city's abominable towman won't be in action today."

- WNEW memo from News Director Mike Stein, December, 1970, slugged "Incidental Intelligence": "Reporter Mike Eisgrau had a marvelous feature on a little old dreidel maker, the lady who makes most of the dreidels sold during the Chanukah season."

I loved working at WNEW, but the station was changing, and not for the better. The newer air personalities, at least in my opinion, weren't in the same league as William B. and others who were there when I arrived in 1967.

The station hired Julius La Rosa. Remember Julie? He was a singer popular in the 1950s—*the* singer famously fired on the air by Arthur Godfrey, who said Julie lacked humility. La Rosa had also hired an agent who irked the "ole redhead," who wanted all of his so-called "little God-freys" under one roof, so he could be in full control of their careers.

I got to know Julie quite well; he was a great guy, but he really seemed out of place at what had been dubbed as "The World's Greatest Radio Station." For the station's 50th anniversary in 1984, a book was published—*WNEW, Where the Melody Lingers On.* It's wonderful, but, sadly, it's mostly about the station's heyday, and by 1984 the melody that "lingered" had lost its resonance. Less than 10 years later, in 1992, WNEW left the airwaves, sold to Michael Bloomberg's company, and that once great Eleven-Three-O spot on the dial was now called WBBR, a news/business station, with ratings that didn't even crack the top 20 in the New York market.

Newsday's Paul Colford put the end of the station this way: "WNEW-AM/1130, the 58-year-old outlet for the music of Frank Sinatra, Lena Horne, Mel Tormé, and America's greatest songwriters, died today after a long illness, marked by financial losses, anemic ratings, schizophrenic programming and the dismissal of practically every personality who made it special." In the end, WNEW's once-great news department was now a shadow of what it once was. "News every half hour around the clock" was no more on WNEW, and of course by then New York had not one but two all-news stations, WINS and WCBS-AM.

Meanwhile, let's go back briefly to my waning days at "The Big W"—WNEW—in 1971. The ratings were down, William B. Williams was complaining that he was being forced to play what was known as "chicken rock," softer rock tunes that wouldn't offend older listeners, and I learned about an opening at a network, ABC. I had always aspired to join a network and I jumped at the opportunity. In the summer of 1971 I was hired as a news correspondent on the ABC Radio Network. My last newscast on WNEW was on the *Make Believe Ballroom*, and Willie B. gave me an on-air send-off. "There he goes, ladies and gentleman, off to some obscure network." And then he added, "But Bill, look at it this way—on your final day here, the stock market is up. That's a harbinger."

Chapter 5

Forbidden Words, and Other Dictates from the News Editor

A BC Radio in 1968 had split into four news networks: the Information Network, with newscasts on the hour; the Entertainment Network, with news on the half hour; the Contemporary Network, news at :55; and the FM Network, news at :15 past the hour. There were news anchors and editors for each network, and while WNEW's newsroom was impressive, ABC's was really large, a beehive of activity, with reporters around the world.

ABC's vice president of news, Tom O'Brien, assigned me a prime slot as the morning newscaster on the "E" Network, short for the badly named, in my view, Entertainment Network. I replaced the veteran Bob Wilson. A few months after I had been at ABC, O'Brien told me that he was very pleased with my air work, anchoring morning newscasts on the network. "We wanted a ballsier voice in the morning,"

The author in the ABC newsroom.

he said. (Ironically at WNEW I had been told by the news director that I was being taken off the morning shift because they wanted someone with a "ballsier" voice.) O'Brien had arrived at ABC in 1962, coming from WINS. In those days the ABC Radio newsroom delivered hourly newscasts to both the network and the local station, WABC. O'Brien inherited a staff of 24 writers who ground out rewrites of wire copy to be read by staff announcers.

O'Brien once told me in a letter, "I cringe when I think how they demeaned the likes of the great Milton Cross (voice of the Metropolitan Opera broadcasts) assigning him to hourly newscasts during DJ Cousin Brucie's WABC rock 'n' roll program." I don't think a tape of this exists but Cross was once reading a local news story and called then New York City Mayor Robert Wagner "Vog-ner." Hard for Milton to forget about opera.

The ABC Radio Network's big star was the great Paul Harvey, whose news and comment, twice a day, was a huge draw for some 1,200 ABC stations.

There was no one quite like Paul Harvey on network radio, and it's safe to say there never will be anyone like

Paul Harvey.

him, commanding such a huge audience. Harvey's broadcasts came out of Chicago. He had no desire to work in New York and rarely paid a visit to our newsroom. Harvey's staccato delivery was unique, and he wrote his own "News and Comment," although in later years his son Paul Junior did the honors. Listeners loved his folksy "The Rest of the Story" tales based on a real-life person or event. Harvey was famous for adding a little drama to his newscasts. Once he said on air, "Elizabeth Taylor fell off a horse; they had to shoot her (dramatic pause) X-rays." Harvey even mentioned me once in a newscast, quoting a story he liked that I had done earlier in the morning.

Besides Tom O'Brien, the ABC Radio News executives included Nick George, the managing editor, who insisted that radio journalists write and deliver the news in a simple, clear, and concise manner. In one of my first days on the air I suddenly felt someone looking over my shoulder as I was hunched over my typewriter pounding out a story I was working on. It was Nick, pipe in his clenched teeth, who sent shivers up my spine when he said, "Are you sure you're going to say that?" It was Nick's welcome to the newbie in the ABC network newsroom, but also his way of keeping everyone on their toes, including me.

Nick was a hard taskmaster, but also a great editor. Mort Crim, a WNEW anchor and correspondent at ABC before I got there, once said that Nick George "taught me more about good radio writing than all my professors. To this day I cannot bring myself to call a ship a *vessel*," which was one of Nick's many rules. ABC correspondent Stan Martyn once joked, "So if I break a blood vessel Nick, should I say I burst a blood ship?" To which Nick replied, "That's not funny, Martyn."

One of Nick George's ME (Managing Editor) notes from 1971 was on "Words." Here's a sample as George put it. "There are a few words you can find in the dictionary that we would rather not use on the air. That's because people . . . good people . . . don't ordinarily use them when they talk to each other. Such words as are listed here are 'no/no's:

> hurled, rampage, ravage, welding, clash, probe, shootout, sniper, within the hour, vessel, lunar, blaze *(as a noun)* accuse *(unless the actual word accused is used by a newsmaker)* charge *(unless there is an actual admission in the legal sense). These are just a few pieces of junk we're better off without. A casual remark, in response to no question even, may become an ADMISSION! Nonsense! We shouldn't degrade our reporting by using words that don't fit.*

It's amazing to me that today words like *sniper, lunar, vessel* or *shootout,* are used all the time in newscasts.

Someone wrote that working in the ABC newsroom during Nick's time was "like living on a verbal fault line. You knew an earthquake was inevitable, you just didn't know when." (Once when I was at the urinal in the men's room, I suddenly heard Nick's voice. He was talking into a tape recorder, and didn't want to forget something important.)

"Going on a bit of vacation," reads one George memo. "A chance to remind, that a situation at Wounded Knee may be as provocative and as interesting as what happens at the Majestic in Paris or on the hill in Washington. What was it Steinbeck once said? 'If a story is not about the hearer . . . he or she will not listen. He is only interested in the deeply personal . . . and the familiar.'" George goes on, "The trouble with reporting BIG news is that the world may change and our listeners would never have known the changes were coming. Be different . . . innovate . . . inform inform . . . don't dull . . . always have a changeup . . . and use simple . . . direct . . . ENGLISH."

Network radio was as unionized as my previous employers. Once in my early days at ABC I was filling up a water pitcher for my studio at the office fountain. "That's my job," said a man who approached me. He was a member of the stagehands' union, and one of his jobs was to make sure the studio water pitchers were refilled. I don't think he filed a grievance; it was just a friendly slap on the wrist.

While I had worked for some big radio stations, WTOP in Washington and WNEW in New York, I was blown away by the huge staff at ABC. There were THREE other people involved when I did a newscast: an editor, a studio engineer, and a director. The director cued me and the engineer on tape inserts in the 'cast, and sometimes had to time me during one commercial. That was because the last :30 second commercial slot within the newscasts did not always have a commercial sold in all time zones, so I had to cover with what was known as a "fill" story. That way there was no dead air in a region where there was no network commercial playing, but I had to finish reading the "fill" at the same time the taped commercials in the other time zones ended.

Back in the old days of radio drama, a director was a key element of a broadcast. Warren Somerville was one of those directors who moved over to ABC News when radio dramas ended. Warren was good friends with Margaret Hamilton (who famously played the Wicked Witch of the West in *The Wizard of Oz*) and Fred Gwynn, of TV's *The Munsters* and *Car 54, Where Are You?* Long before I arrived at ABC in 1971, Telly Savalas was an ABC radio director. Yep, the same Telly Savalas who was an actor in a number of 1960s films but perhaps became best known for the 1970s crime drama *Kojak*. I never had a chance to meet Telly, but if I did I would have wanted to ask him about his days as an ABC radio director.

By the mid-80s, most studio engineers and all directors had been phased out in union negotiations, and news correspondents were running their own control boards during newscasts and editing their own interviews. Also by then, satellites were in full use and stations were getting 'casts and programs via "the bird" and of course commercials, too, that could easily be fed to different time zones.

Although I was hired as a news correspondent at ABC Radio I was also able to do several interview programs, *Meet the Newsmaker* and *Meet the Author* were two of them. Often, happily, these interviews were with celebrities.

One of my first big celebrity interviews at ABC was with "The King of Swing," Benny Goodman, on his

Left to right: Benny Goodman, Mike Stein, Tom O'Brien and Bill Diehl.

64th birthday, May 30, 1973. In the mid-1930s Goodman led one of the most popular music groups in America. His concert at New York's Carnegie Hall on January 16, 1938, was described by music critic Bruce Eder as "the single most important jazz or popular music concert in history: jazz's 'coming out' party in the world of respectable music."

I began my interview by asking Goodman if he would ever retire. "No," he said. "I guess I'm the 'Chairman of the Board' [a line often used by WNEW's William B. Williams to describe Frank Sinatra]; I can retire when I want to." Goodman continued to perform until nearly the end of his life. He died at 77 on June 13, 1986.

Goodman told me he rarely listened to his music at home, saying he enjoyed classical music a lot. During the taping of our program, *Meet the Newsmaker*, we played some of The Beatles' music and Goodman said he liked a good many of their songs, like "Yesterday" and a silly one

called "Octopus's Garden," written and sung by Ringo
Starr, credited to his real name, Richard Starkey. Goodman said it reminded him of a song called "Minnie the
Mermaid." Goodman wasn't a fan of some of The Beatles'
other music, which he felt was often noisy and too loud. He
did say that he took his daughter Rachel to see The Beatles
perform at the Forest Hills Stadium in New York in August
1964. Two years earlier Goodman had played in Russia to
an audience of ten thousand.

During an era of segregation in America, Goodman
led one of the first well-known integrated jazz groups. Asked
about his greatest influences in music, Goodman singled
out Louis Armstrong, the New Orleans Rhythm Kings, and
Bix Beiderbecke, the American jazz cornetist, jazz pianist,
and composer. Along with Armstrong and Muggsy Spanier,
Beiderbecke was one of the most influential jazz soloists of
the 1920s. Goodman's philosophy of life? Benny Goodman
said, "I do the best I can and try to play well. I always feel
it's opening night."

If ever there was a man for all seasons, it was Steve
Allen: talk-show host, musician, composer, author, and

Steve Allen.

actor. Allen, who died in October of 2000, did it all, and then some. Allen claimed to have written over 1,000 songs, the best known being "This Could Be the Start of Something Big." It replaced the original opening theme for Allen's shows on NBC including the first *Tonight Show*. It was used until Allen left the show in 1957, replaced by Jack Paar. While Allen got his start in radio, he was best known for his television career.

Asked about embarrassing moments, Allen said it was the time when he was doing a radio show. Peggy Lee was his guest, and when she finished singing and got a standing ovation, "I looked out at the audience and one guy wasn't clapping. So I jumped off the stage and took my microphone into the audience, zeroing in on this guy and why he didn't applaud. But then as I got real close I discovered, much to my dismay, that he had no hands. I quickly turned to the lady sitting next to him and asked a silly question about what was in her pocketbook."

Allen recalled another memorable incident, this one on television with John Cameron Swayze, who was doing one of his famous Timex watch commercials—"It takes a licking and keeps on ticking." It was live, and the watch had been attached to the blade of a motorboat inside a plastic water tank. When it started up, water splashed all over the studio and, to Swayze's shock, the watch disappeared. Allen remembers Swayze couldn't say anything except, "We'll be back next week. And I said, 'If there *is* a next week.' Swayze didn't talk to me for a while after that line."

I told Allen that he was sort of a household word. "So is Drano, but if you're on television, it's so powerful that it makes you seem important, whether you are or not. If I were doing a show now I could take a cucumber and take a close-up of it every night for ten nights and I can assure you the cucumber would begin to get fan mail. It would be in

Time magazine as the most famous cucumber. It's nothing but a stupid cucumber, but now it's famous."

Often when interviewing celebrities, I would ask about being remembered. When I asked Allen how he wanted people to remember him when he's gone, he said "Oh, about every 20 minutes." Allen said that when he thought about leaving the planet he recalled what Danny Thomas once said when his father was dying. "His father's last words, and since we're on radio I'll have to use a euphemism, he said, 'G. death.'"

I miss Steve Allen; he had a wonderful wit, able to move from the heaviest and complex subjects to crazy comedy. Once, when he arrived at my studio, he had a tiny tape recorder in his hand. "What's that for?" I asked. Allen said, "I might say something great, providing raw material I can use later on."

Chapter 6

How to Talk
Like a Newsman

While showbiz interviews were fun, my main job was as a newscaster and occasionally a field reporter at ABC. Vice president of news Tom O'Brien was a stickler for what he considered good newswriting. A memo from 1976 said, "Let's not be vague! Our listeners deserve to know the 'who, what, where and how' of every story." O'Brien pointed to a newscast script that described a summit conference taking place at a "famous Puerto Rican hotel," ignoring the fact that it was the Dorado Beach.

And yet we could not say on the air "The Macy's Thanksgiving Day Parade." O'Brien felt it was a free commercial for Macy's, even though it was Macy's parade. So when we did a story on the parade we had to say "The Thanksgiving Day Parade in New York." Another newscast spoke of President Gerald Ford and Governor Jimmy Carter "at a political dinner," ignoring the important fact that it was New York's annual Al Smith dinner, traditionally nonpartisan, meaning those then—presidential candidates could not make strong political speeches. It was that atmosphere that kept everyone on edge, living under a critical eye in the ABC Radio newsroom.

Here's another example. In 1975, President Ford traveled to China; O'Brien, as ABC Radio's news chief, went along too. He brought with him his shortwave radio. When he returned to New York he handed me a recording on cassette. On it was my ABC newscast as broadcast on Armed Forces Radio shortwave, with O'Brien saying, "I'm listening to Bill Diehl coming across the Gobi Desert." There had been a glitch in my cast when a piece of tape didn't play. Said O'Brien, "that's what rehearsals are for, Willie." O'Brien wanted newscasters in the studio, unless it was an emergency situation, five minutes before airtime, so we could rehearse the tape inserts with the studio engineer and director.

O'Brien also wanted his correspondents to dress properly, always have at least a sport coat and tie handy. Once he popped in on a weekend and saw one of his newscasters in shorts. "Heading to the beach?" he said. The next day a memo came out in which O'Brien stressed that correspondents should always be dressed nicely in case they were called out to cover a story. They were representing ABC News, and he wanted them to look it.

There was a lot of ribbing and jokes behind O'Brien's ample back; he got the nickname "The Pumpkin," because of the shape of his big head. On one side of the newsroom was a huge map with lights that lit up for different cities around the world. When a guest was coming to the newsroom O'Brien's secretary would flip a switch under her desk and the map would light up. Sitting nearby you could feel the heat from it.

Once, correspondent Bob Walker and I got into an argument. I can't remember what it was about, but he hurled a paper cup of coffee at me. It missed and coffee splattered onto the big map smack on the Mariana Islands in the South Pacific, leaving a permanent brown stain. From then on, Walker would sometimes mock threaten me that "It'll Be Coffee Time in the Marianas," a phrase that became a newsroom legend.

Correspondent Don Blair took some heat in another way when he got in trouble for doing a story on the network about a product he had invested in. When Blair found out he was getting the boot, he did not go quietly . . . in fact he did it quite publicly . . . on the air, no less. In his final newscast, instead of saying the tag "a service of ABC News," Blair said, "a CIRCUS of ABC News." Somebody went to

The author with correspondent Bob Walker, in front of the newsroom's big map. (Photo by Bill Stoller)

O'Brien's office saying, "Did you hear what Blair just said on the air?" O'Brien came rushing out of his office to confront Blair but he was too late. Blair had his coat with him and was out of the studio and down the elevator to Broadway.

Blair headed to the bar at The Saloon next door. At which point, he told me, "I was ordering a double Manhattan and sitting next to the great Fred Foy, the ABC announcer. After I told him what I had just done, Fred said, 'Yes, I'd order one of those too.'" Meanwhile, back upstairs in the newsroom, O'Brien was heard saying about Blair's stunt, "He'll never work in this town again." Undaunted, Blair headed to NBC News and was hired almost immediately by Bob Kimmel. "When I told him what I had done, Kimmel said 'Well, we'll judge you by what you do here.'"

The author with Howard Cosell.

Blair, now in his 80s, told me, "At least folks remember me for something." Truth be told, Don Blair did well at NBC Radio News, spending 15 productive years at 30 Rock.

Also on the ABC staff was Howard Cosell, who was on television as well as radio when I arrived at ABC. Like Paul Harvey, who was worth millions in advertising dollars to ABC, Cosell had lots of clout—so much so that broadcast lines were installed in his Upper East Side Manhattan apartment and at Cosell's house in suburban Westchester County, so he could do his twice daily *Speaking of Sports* programs without coming to our studios every day. (And a tech went with him when he was traveling for football games and other events.) Before Cosell would start taping from home, he would do a "talk up" with an engineer in an ABC control room.

Howard was known to *kibbitz* before going on and the engineer often had a tape rolling. "How are you today, Howard?" the engineer might ask. And Howard might say, "I just don't know; this is too much for me to contemplate." The engineer would then give this and other Howard "outtakes" to Dan Ingram, the afternoon DJ at WABC radio. And just before Howard would come on with his sportscast, Ingram might say, "Howard Cosell is coming up shortly with sports. How's it going. Howard?" And Ingram's engineer would play one of the outtakes. One time, Ingram began saying, "This is a first, everyone—the singing debut of Howard Cosell." And then Howard began: "I left my heart in San Francisco. High on hill [he misses a few words in the lyrics] where little cable cars climb halfway to the stars."

In another outtake played on Ingram's show, Cosell is heard singing, "For once in my life I found someone who needs me, someone who knows how to care. Once in my life I was in love with a horse." But the talk-up taping with Howard came to an abrupt end. Eddie Salzman, an engineer at the network, told me that before Howard began taping his show, "I would start recording him to make sure everything was working. One time Howard was talking about Frank Gifford and was not saying very complimentary things about him. I thought it was pretty funny. Later I played the tape back for some other engineers, who also thought it was funny. What I didn't know was he was still in his Manhattan apartment and heard the tape playback on a speaker there. From then on it was downhill. His wife, Emmy, got involved and demanded that the tape and any copies be erased." Eddie wasn't sure if Emmy actually came to the studio, but from then on, engineers were told to end any taping that was not of the Cosell show itself.

Cosell did come to the studios sometimes to tape his afternoon program, and to tape his longer weekly *Speaking of Everything*, with guests.

I liked Howard. He was a real character. In his later years, he had the office next to mine, and would often come by to shoot the breeze. By then, however, "The Coach," as he was dubbed, was no longer the big star that he once had been, and when Emmy died, the Howard Cosell we used to know was not in evidence anymore. It was sad to see.

I interviewed Cosell in 1991 for his fourth book, *What's Wrong with Sports*, co-written with ABC Radio Sports Director Shelby Whitfield. I told Cosell that over the years, he had been called "arrogant" and "obnoxious." Did it ever get to him? "Of course it has; I'm human, but only if it's from someone I respect." But he quickly added that he had said that laughingly at a function in California, "It was clear I was joking but the press ran with it." Asked if he felt he had left a major mark on sports, Cosell said, "How can you question that? You know very well that I have. There will not ever be another like me; sports journalism is dead."

Early on at the ABC Radio network, two of the star anchors on the Eyewitness News Team at Channel 7, WABC-TV, Roger Grimsby and Bill Beutel, also did newscasts on radio. I got to know Grimsby quite well and loved his acerbic humor. When Roger died in 1995, Ron Tindiglia, who had been Channel 7's news director, spoke at a memorial service and recalled when Howard Cosell was still doing local TV sports as well as having his network radio programs on ABC. Tindiglia said, "Cosell seemed jealous of Roger for some reason and on the throwback to him after his sportscast he would say things sarcastically like 'Now, here he is, the anchorman that was a big success in San Francisco and now is gracing us with his presence in New York.'

"It was cutting stuff, but Roger was ready for it. Never showing any facial expression, Roger said after one such throwback, 'You know Howard, I don't mind being your pigeon since you are such a big statute in the sports world.' Then he stopped cold and just stared at the camera until the director faded to black and went to commercials.'"

Tindiglia didn't mention it, but one time after a Cosell throwback, Grimsby said, "If words were birds, Howard, you'd be covered in white." No love lost between those two.

When I arrived at ABC in 1971, our radio studios were on the fifth floor at 1926 Broadway, across from Lincoln Center, an old parking garage built in the early 1900s when that part of Broadway was "Automobile Row," with car showrooms and offices. 1972 was an election year, and ABC Radio went all out, sending me and other network correspondents to Miami Beach to cover both the Republican and Democratic conventions there. We had a full studio constructed and did our morning newscasts from Miami.

I should also note that 1972 was special on a very personal level. It was the year our daughter, Suzanne Carroll

Bill Diehl on the Democratic Convention floor.

Diehl, was born. Her birth made the showbiz bible *Variety*. It marked another wonderful milestone in my life.

I also covered political conventions in 1976 in Kansas City and New York and was often out on the convention floor doing interviews.

There were horrible floods along the Mississippi in the early 1970s, and in 1973 I was sent to Missouri, from which I fed reports to the entire network. In 1977 I covered George Willig's climb up the north tower of the World Trade Center in New York. Via a shortwave transmitter I did a live broadcast from the roof of the Trade Center's south tower to capture a good view of Willig's ascent to the top.

In those days, when our newscast air shift ended it was expected that we would go out and cover a story. ABC's assignment editor, Martin Bush, once told me to go to the Waldorf Astoria for a chemical workers' convention. When I told him this was a totally alien world for me, he replied "Bill, think of yourself as a lone fighter pilot, I'm sure you'll find something." I did, but doubt it ever was used on air.

Part II

Memorable Moments: Talking with the Stars

Chapter 7

From Audrey Hepburn to Marilyn Chambers: Early Interviews

As I said, while I was hired to mainly do newscasts at ABC, I was also given the opportunity to do celebrity interviews, including talking with some of the biggest stars in the business—among them, Jerry Lewis, Jane Fonda, and Robin Williams. Eventually I also got a regular feature program, called *Bill Diehl's Spotlight*, which was available to affiliate stations three times a week. Here are some nuggets from those interviews.

A FEW SHORT TAKES

Tony Curtis

Tony Curtis, born Bernard Schwartz, had a career that spanned six decades, although he was most popular during the 1950s and early '60s, acting in more than 100 films. One of my favorites was *Some Like it Hot,* with Jack Lemmon and Marilyn Monroe. What was it like to kiss Monroe? I asked. To my surprise and disappointment, Curtis said, "It was like kissing cement."

Audrey Hepburn

I was covering an event in which Audrey Hepburn was promoting her work as a United Nations ambassador for UNICEF. I arrived late and had to sit on the floor in front of the podium where Hepburn was speaking. No time to place my mic on the podium, so I had to stretch my arm with the mic as close as I could get. Wish I had a photo of this. Hepburn looked down and said, "You poor boy, let me hold your microphone"—and she did, much to the amazement of other reporters in the room.

Roy Rogers

Once I got word that Roy Rogers was at our TV center a few blocks away. I raced over and persuaded Roy's manager to

have "The King of the Cowboys" do an interview with me at our nearby ABC radio studio. Picture this: me with Rogers, in full cowboy regalia, walking along Broadway, turning heads from passersby as we made our way to the studio. Rogers, who began his show business career in California in 1930, said he was "starved into it" by the Depression. After working the peach orchards of Northern California, he headed south. "I couldn't find a job so I went on a little amateur radio station and I sang and played the guitar and mandolin and yodeled. About three days later a fellow called and I joined a group called The Rocky Mountain Airs. A couple of years later I formed The Sons of the Pioneers." In my interview Rogers said he was surprised his popularity had lasted for so many years. "It may be that I'm more than just a cowboy, that I'm more like a member of the family." In light of what's happening now it's interesting that in this 1981 interview Rogers said he believes screen violence is unnecessary, that films are often making police officers look foolish and these are people our kids used to look up to. Rogers voiced his belief that gun control will not be the answer for today's violent society. "I am not for gun control, because it won't control the people who get guns anyway. The day there is gun control in this country, it's going to be really chaotic." Remember Roy Rogers said this to me 35 years ago!

Christie Brinkley
And then there was Christie Brinkley. Can't remember the reason for the interview, but I've got this photo of Brinkley playfully grabbing my mic and trying to interview me.

Paul Hogan

Paul Hogan of *Crocodile Dundee* fame: Was he surprised by his success? "Yeah, I'm kind of like a Cinderella in boots."

David Crosby

As a founding member of The Byrds, David Crosby helped pioneer the folk-rock genre. Crosby, Stills and Nash's self-titled 1969 debut album was an immediate hit. The group won the Best New Artist Grammy. Songs on that debut album included a Crosby-penned classic, "Long Time Gone."

I told David Crosby, you're a legend. And Crosby said, "That's silly. I put my pants on one leg at a time the same as you." So you don't care what they say about you a hundred years from now when you'll probably be gone? "I won't be around so it won't matter to me. There is certainly nobody that has gotten into as much trouble as I have."

Daphne du Maurier and Barbara Cartland

I traveled to England in 1973. It was mostly for vacation but included some interviews with authors Daphne du Maurier (*Jamaica Inn, Rebecca,* and other novels) and romance novelist Barbara Cartland. At first Cartland's editor in New York told me she wasn't doing interviews but I could write a letter to her, which I did. It hit the right note when I said I noted her interest in the environment and her membership in Britain's National Trust.

Du Maurier had invited my wife and me to lunch at her home in Cornwall, followed by an interview, the first she had ever done with an American broadcaster. I told her that she had once been quoted as saying that human selfishness is the root of all the trouble in the world. Did she still believe that? "I think it's still true, but I don't think there's any cure for it." Asked about writing, "It's like having a baby, once it's printed and I get my first copy, it's over. I never look back." Ever think she would stop writing? "When you get tired of life," she said "then the ideas stop coming." There was a television set at her home but du Maurier said she was fed up with watching too many naked shoulders. "I would rather watch a documentary about how to preserve seals or something about butterflies."

Barbara Cartland, famous for her devotion to the color pink, had her chauffeur pick us up at our London hotel in her white Rolls-Royce to take us to her estate in Hertfordshire, north of the city. Quite a treat—we had never had a ride in a Rolls-Royce, complete with a pink mohair rug in the backseat for extra comfort. The interview went well, Cartland chatting as she held her dog on her lap. Cartland's novels, quite tame with virginal heroines, contained no sex, violence, or profanity. She told me "I think pornography is vulgar, disgusting and degrading to woman." In her stories, as she put it, "people don't roll around naked." As for the characters she wrote about, "I'm always in love with the heroes in my books. They're much easier because I can shut them up, can't I."

A CELEBRITY MOSAIC

Bernadette Peters

One of my favorite female singers is Bernadette Peters. Born Bernadette Lazzara to a Sicilian-American family in

Ozone Park, New York, she took the name Peters to avoid ethnic stereotyping. Peters has done it all—film, television, theater, concerts, and she's a two-time Tony Award winner. We had a delightful chat when she paid a visit to my ABC studio. I began our interview by reminding her of a song she sang called "When You're Making Love Alone." Peters said she was going to sing it on *Saturday Night Live,* but NBC censors weren't so sure it would be appropriate, because it's a song about masturbation. Finally, they relented, and she sang it. Peters is a favorite singer of Stephen Sondheim. I asked her, what is it about her relationship with Sondheim? She said, "I just love the way he writes and the way he can pick a subject and get the essence of what he wants to say in song."

I told her that a music critic once said Peters manages to spoof the idea of a pop diva even if she's playing the role to the hilt. "I never heard that before, but I remember I once saw Elvis Presley perform. He came out and my mouth dropped open. I wasn't even that big a fan, and I thought, *this is what they mean by a superstar.* He was going to sing 'Blue Suede Shoes' and he gets down and kind of crouches in front of the microphone and says, 'I gotta get in position for this.' And he was laughing at himself. And I thought, *that's so great to have a sense of humor about yourself.*"

Peters once posed for Vargas, the Peruvian painter who was famous for his pin-up girls. "He was 84, but I persuaded him to do a Vargas-girl portrait of me. I joked, 'We're gonna be arrested here.' But I loved it and had the original framed." Painted in 1980, Bernadette Peters was his last Vargas-girl portrait. He died two years later.

See the interview here:
https://youtu.be/ohwMv2PKs8A

Barbra Streisand

What can I say about the truly amazing Barbra Streisand? Once I was on Manhattan's West Side and someone had a bunch of VHS tapes on a table. One of them said Streisand. I bought it for two bucks. Clearly the owner had been a huge fan. The tape included one of Streisand's first appearances on TV. It was 1962's *Garry Moore Show,* and Moore said, "for anybody who has been in the business as long as I have this is the advent of a bright new young star." Moore introduced 19-year-old Streisand who was currently in the Broadway show *I Can Get It for You Wholesale,* and "stopped the show cold," as he put it. He also mentioned that Streisand could be seen nightly at a club in Greenwich Village called "The Bon Soir." I had not seen this old black-and-white show before and Streisand was a knockout singing "When the Sun Comes Out." She sent shivers up my spine.

I've seen Streisand in person a couple of times over the years, including in 1991 when I was part of a small group of reporters interviewing her for her film *The Prince of Tides,* which she directed and starred in. Streisand talked about the film of course but also her earliest days, growing up in Brooklyn and as a teenager watching *Your Hit Parade* on TV and singing songs that were featured. At first she said she wanted to be an actress, but, "I was a kid who had a good voice in the neighborhood so I started to sing because I couldn't get work acting. I knew if I did well I could get a job to pay rent that way, so I sang and got famous as a singer on Broadway."

When I asked her what it was that has always kept her going she said, "I like challenges. I seem to have grown up with them. It seems to be part of my nature." Then she turned more personal. "People can heal the pain of their childhood. I believe that we all want to forgive. It's a wonderful feeling to let go of anger. It makes you a richer person, a happier person, to become a mature adult and have some distance and consciousness to go back to your past and really breathe and rediscover the pure self that you are and not think you're so awful because you were told you were awful and not live other people's opinions of you. Discover that true child, that true self so you can embrace all parts of yourself."

As I write this, Barbra Streisand, at 74, has been getting rave reviews and sold-out crowds as she embarks on yet another tour, called *Barbra: The Music...The Mem'ries...The Magic!* And there's another album of duets, *Encore: Movie Partners Sing Broadway*, her 35th studio album. Years ago I covered what was being called her "farewell tour" at Madison Square Garden. She was fabulous and the audience went wild. But of course that wasn't a farewell. Barbra Streisand keeps coming back, reinventing herself. She's the musical engine that keeps on giving, and we're the better for it.

Christopher Reeve

Christopher Reeve was a guest in my studio in 1993. In May of 1995 Reeve broke his neck while riding a horse in an exhibition in Virginia. It was chilling to go back to the tape of that interview and hear Reeve talking about the dangers of jumping while riding his horse. He conceded it could be dangerous, but said he was confident that he was trained well in the sport. At the time, Reeve was living with Gae Exton, a model. Why no marriage? I asked. "It's all based on the idea of commitment, and if you know you're committed you know the commitment is there and it won't be affected by a piece of paper."

Our conversation turned to Superman, a role in which he had been so identified. Was he worried about being tagged with the Superman label? "Oh, yeah. The public will sometimes see me in this way—Christopher (Superman) Reeve, just like Robin (Mork) Williams, Howard (Humble Howard) Cosell, even Muhammad (the Greatest) Ali. Everyone has a kind of label. But because we live in an age of media hype, media identification, that's all part of the ballgame, and who cares?" Reeve made one more comment about playing Superman on screen. "I knocked myself out to make Superman come alive," Reeve had told *Newsweek*. "People will say 'Are you Superman?' I say, 'No, but I've got his phone number. I'm his mouthpiece right now, that's all.'"

Hugh Hefner

"Hi, Bill, how would you like to meet Hugh Hefner at the Playboy Mansion?" It was the spring of 2000, and Bill Farley, the mansion's publicist, was on the phone with the invitation, and of course I said yes. I was in L.A. covering the Academy Awards, but had the afternoon free, so I drove over to the mansion in the swanky Holmby Hills neighborhood. There was "Hef" on hand to greet me in his burgundy smoking jacket. I got the grand tour, including the grotto

where, as the stories went, movie stars cavorted with half-naked women, and there was a mini-zoo in the backyard complete with flamingoes and a monkey who was hanging out in a tree. Hef introduced me to twins Mandy and Sandy, who were living with him then. I also met his personal chef.

Hugh Hefner, as you may know, inaugurated *Playboy* in 1953 with its now-famous nude photo of Marilyn Monroe. Hef had gotten $8,000 from investors, along with $1,000 from his mother, to start the magazine, which became an instant hit. After his first marriage ended in 1959, Hefner led a swinger's lifestyle with an ever-changing parade of girlfriends. In 1989 he married Playmate of the Year Kimberly Conrad. The couple, who had two children, split in 1998, and in 2012, at the age of 86, Hefner married his third wife, 26-year-old Crystal Harris. In my interview with Hefner at the mansion I asked him about being remembered. Did he think he'd made a difference? "I like to think I have made a difference," he said, "and I had an awfully good time doing it."

Alan Alda

Alan Alda was a delight to interview. He talked about movies and, of course, M*A*S*H, the hit TV series, in which he played Hawkeye Pierce. Alda's rise to fame didn't come easily. "I was a cab driver, a doorman, and a clown. I had a family to support and I was a young, out of work actor." But he maintained that he wouldn't change anything if given a chance to start over. "There have been a few difficult moments, but they're a lot easier to get through if you are confident that things will turn out great and end like this."

Marilyn Chambers

One of my most bizarre assignments was to interview a porn star, Marilyn Chambers. Procter & Gamble had found out that the fresh-faced young woman who was on the Ivory Snow box was less than 99 and 44 one hundredth percent pure.

Chambers was starring in the X-rated film *Behind the Green Door*. I was sent to the Pussycat Cinema in Times Square to interview Ms. Chambers. Her manager ushered me inside, but the only way I could talk to her, he said, was while she was on a platform, signing autographs. And she was stark naked! A Reuters photographer took a picture of me interviewing Chambers.

The ABC assignment desk was also responsible for sending me to the Jacob Javits convention center, where *The Erotica Show: A Show About Love* was going on. Among the people I interviewed was a man named George Urban, who was also known as Ugly George.

Ugly George

George roamed the streets of Manhattan in an open-chested silver vest and shorts, wearing a big backpack with an antenna and videotaping gear. His trademark come-on to women was, "Let's flex into a dimly lit hallway or come up to my Polish Penthouse." There, if he got lucky, he would urge them to undress and videotape them for later showing on his cable TV show called *The Ugly George Hour of Truth, Sex and Violence.*

Ugly George became a sort of cult figure; he even interviewed John Lennon and Michael Jackson. I interviewed him for ABC at the show, but made the mistake of giving him my business card. A few days later the guard at our reception desk called me in the newsroom and said, "Mr. Diehl, there is a Mr. Ugly George here to see you." Yikes! No way was I going to invite him up to our newsroom. So I went down to the lobby, and there he was, in his full regalia. He presented me with a publicity packet featuring lots of his clippings. I thanked him and said that if we decided to do more stories on erotica, I would get in touch with him.

William Shatner and Leonard Nimoy

What's not to like, interviewing William Shatner and Leonard Nimoy, best known for their *Star Trek* roles on TV and in movies? In a 1987 interview I asked Shatner, Captain Kirk on *Star Trek*, whether, if it were possible, he would like to fast-forward and live in the future. Shatner said, "My only regret is the lure and mystery of the future. If a tree falls in the forest and we don't see it, will there be any mystery beyond my lifetime? Of course there will be, but I won't be there to see it, and that's the lure of science fiction." Asked about the *Star Trek* conventions, Shatner said that at first he shunned them, but then started to go, and realized that people were there to have fun and be entertained. "My presence became a stand-up comedy routine. I had stories, took questions, and it was a spontaneous act and I made them laugh."

Leonard Nimoy, of course, played Mr. Spock on *Star Trek*. Was it a problem, being so identified with Spock?

Nimoy said it really had not been as much of a problem as people might think, though in fan mail, writers often tried to tell him what he should do. "But I can't live my life that way. There's an old saying, 'Everybody has businesses—their own and show business.' In my case, I guess some try to run two lives, their own and mine." When I said that people who see him sometimes expect he'll have pointy ears like his Spock character, Nimoy admitted he gets people with bad ear jokes from time to time. "I've had enough of those to last me a lifetime." Nimoy died in 2015 at the age of 83.

Robin Williams

Getting an interview with Robin Williams took some doing. I heard he was appearing at Catch a Rising Star, a popular stand-up-comedy club on Manhattan's Upper East Side. I went there and met his manager. I told him I would love to have Williams come to our ABC Radio network studios. He said it was unlikely, because Robin was very busy. But he took my business card and said he would pass it on to Robin.

The next day I'm at my desk in the newsroom and the phone rings. "Hi, Bill, this is Robin Williams. Do you still want to do the interview?" "Of course!" Then Robin said, "I'll be over in about 20 minutes." This was 1982, and *Mork and Mindy* had just ended on ABC- TV; now Williams was promoting an HBO special. It was a memorable interview, with Robin being Robin, alternately serious about himself and his career but also treating me to terrific impressions, including actors Peter Lorre and Jack Nicholson. He even did some funny promos for my show, *Bill Diehl's Spotlight;* it was all off-the-cuff, and he was hilarious. Oh, yes—as he was leaving our studio, he asked if we could give him some carfare to take him back to his hotel. One of our assistants, Andrea Berken, remembers it well. She gave him five dollars.

Kenny Rogers

Years earlier, I had interviewed cowboy singer Roy Rogers, and another singing Rogers who graced my ABC microphone was Kenny Rogers. "I'm trying to be as unpredictable within a framework of consistency as I can," said Rogers of his singing success. "I think it would be foolish of me to do drug songs one week and religious songs the next. Rogers began his career in the late '60s with the soft-rock group The First Edition. When the group broke up after 10 years in 1975, Rogers turned to country and western music. One year later he scored with a hit song: "Lucille." In a 1981 interview, Rogers acknowledged that he thought the song was trite. "It was everything you'd try to stay away from in music, yet the minute I heard it I knew it was going to be a major success." Rogers talked about his philosophy of success in the music business. "Give us a little success and we'll make a lot out of you," he said. "I feel my strength has always been surrounding myself with professional people that really do the work. The trick is not only to surround yourself with them but let them do their work." And then he added, "I don't think I'm a particularly good singer, but I'm getting better, and the more hits I have, the more I start taking myself seriously."

Xaviera Hollander

Xaviera Hollander's book *The Happy Hooker* was her story about becoming the most famous and successful madam in New York City. But, she told me, "Mine is not a house of ill-repute. It is a house of pleasure."

Xaviera was bursting with charm when I interviewed her in a brownstone apartment in 1981 for an ABC feature we were doing on prostitution; it was then getting lots of attention from city officials. Hollander signed the book with these words: "Dear Bill, may you enjoy this educational book. Learn and practice now, keep in touch with the Dutch"—a reference to her homeland, the Netherlands.

Chapter 8

More Stars, from Lauren Bacall to Gérard Depardieu

Lauren Bacall

Lauren Bacall, born Betty Joan Perske, went from part-time fashion model to one of the screen's leading ladies. "You know how to whistle, don't you, Steve? You just put your lips together and blow." Bacall was just 19 when she said that line to Humphrey Bogart in *To Have and Have Not*.

When I asked Bacall in a 1996 interview about the whistle line, she told me, "It had a tremendous impact at the time. It just connected and I suppose that movie was one of the reasons that I became a star so quickly." Their chemistry was such that when Bogie and Bacall were next cast in *The Big Sleep*, the film that was partially rewritten to exploit the notoriety of their relationship, Bogart was married and 25 years her senior. They married a year later.

The couple starred together in only two more movies: *Dark Passage* and *Key Largo*, but their marriage became one of Hollywood's great love stories.

In 1953 Bacall appeared in her first comedy, *How to Marry a Millionaire*. She continued acting after Bogart died in 1957. On Broadway she won Tony Awards for *Applause* in 1970 and *Woman of the Year* in 1981. She scored a supporting Oscar nod in 1996 for *The Mirror Has Two Faces*, which starred Barbra Streisand. In 2006, at the age of 82, Bacall had a cameo on TV's *The Sopranos*.

And oh, yes, the American Film Institute voted her one of the 25 most significant female movie stars in history. When I asked her about being remembered for her achievements, she said, "I don't know, I don't think in those terms. I guess because I don't want to think about not being around." She laughed. But when I pursued that subject again, saying, "So you don't care what they say about you fifty or a hundred years from now?" She laughed again and said, "How will I know?" When I met her again at a 50th anniversary celebration for *Casablanca* at New York's Lincoln Center, I mentioned that there was a rumor about doing a remake of *Casablanca*. Without missing a beat, Bacall said, "Why the fuck would they?"

Mickey Rooney

Mickey Rooney was a huge box office star in the 1930s and '40s in the Andy Hardy series and films with Judy Garland. But even when he was much older, he appeared on Broadway and in a few more films, including *A Night at the Museum*. In my chat with "the Mick," as he often called himself, he said he never worried about growing old. "Age is nothing but experience, and some of us have more experience than others. I think the word *senior citizen* is a bummer. It connotes that you're decadent and over the hill."

How did he want to be remembered? "Just as a fella who tried. I don't know what kind of a record will ever be left or whether the record is important to be left at all. But I love people. I've loved the opportunity of being able to do what God has let me do, and that's what I've tried to do the best I can."

Billy Crystal

Billy Crystal has been one of my favorite people to interview. First famous as a stand-up comedian and cast member of *Saturday Night Live*, Billy became a Hollywood star in the late 1980s and into the '90s, appearing in films like *When Harry Met Sally, City Slickers, Analyze This*, and a 1995 film, *Forget Paris*.

Crystal told me that "any good romantic comedy should have a happy ending." Part of *Forget Paris* was shot in The City of Light, and I asked Crystal if he has fans there. "One guy told me he likes me better than Jerry Lewis." Crystal does some great impressions, including Muhammad Ali (he did some of it at the memorial service for Ali) and Howard Cosell. I also love his comic impression of actor

Fernando Lamas, as a smarmy talk show host who had the catchphrase "You look mahvelous!"

(There's a video of the interview at https://www. youtube.com/watch?v=U3j-qNCo-iw& feature=youtu.be.)

In 1989 Crystal performed at the Pushkin Theater, in Moscow, to a mixed audience of foreign diplomats and Soviets. It became an HBO special, *Midnight Train to Moscow*. Crystal didn't see himself as an American ambassador; he said, "I was my family's ambassador." Crystal's mother's family originally came from Moscow, and his father's from the then Soviet city of Odessa. Back in New York, Crystal told me, "They asked me to come back, and said, 'Are there others like you?' I told them, 'Plenty.' They got a kick out of me, and made me feel great."

The opening minutes of his act were delivered in Russian. He studied Russian for two months with the same teacher who worked with Robin Williams for his movie *Moscow on the Hudson*. I covered the Academy Awards many times, and my favorite host was Billy Crystal, who did the Oscars 8 times. But he doesn't hold the record, far from it. Bob Hope hosted a record 18 times. Johnny Carson comes in third at 5 times.

Arnold Schwarzenegger and Rachel McLish

Not only did I interview a Mr. Olympia, but Ms. Olympia too. The Mr. was none other than Arnold Schwarzenegger. The Ms. was Rachel McLish, who at the time was one of the most famous female body builders. And Arnold, of course, became one of the most important figures in the history of body building.

I interviewed him twice, once at a hotel for the film *Conan the Barbarian*, and again in our studio at ABC for *Predator*. McLish had a connection to Schwarzenegger.

She had co-starred with him in a fitness video called "Shape Up." Schwarzenegger was a pussycat in both of my interviews, enjoying his celebrity, although when I asked him if he saw himself as a sex symbol, he said, "That's not the bottom line. My bottom line is to do great movies that are a hit at the box office."

Did he ever think he would become so famous and have a star on the Hollywood Walk of Fame? "That's very nice, because when I first came to this country [from Austria] I remember I wanted to see Hollywood. It was the place I had heard so much about. And when my friends took me there to Hollywood Boulevard and I saw those stars on the pavement I had heard so much about, I thought, wouldn't it be great to have my star on Hollywood Boulevard. You don't even dream about it, so far-fetched, but then I got one, and there I am right next to Judy Garland. What a great experience."

Schwarzenegger said that when he got into acting, "I thought I wanted to be another Clint Eastwood, that there was room at the top of that ladder for me to move in. But it was hard work, taking a lot of acting classes, working on my voice and accent. It was fortunate that action movies were in, adventure films, and people were asking for actors who looked heroic, and that's why my films have done so well."

This was before Schwarzenegger got into politics and became governor of California. When I asked him what he thought film historians would say about him a hundred years later, he said, "With my star on the Walk of Fame, they'll remember me because I'm cemented in. All I'll have to do," he joked, "is hire someone to clean my gold star." Anything he would change? "No, and at the same time I have to give this country a lot of credit for it. I don't think a lot of these things would have happened to me if I had not come to America. It's still the country of opportunities. You can come here, and if you work hard you can make it."

Sylvester Stallone

Sylvester Gardenzio Stallone, like Schwarzenegger, made his mark in action movies, particularly as boxer Rocky Balboa, the title character in the *Rocky* film series. In 1977 Stallone was nominated for two Academy Awards for *Rocky*: Best Original Screenplay and Best Actor. He became only the third man in history to receive these two nominations for the same film, after Charlie Chaplin and Orson Welles. This photo with Stallone was taken at the New York launch party for Planet Hollywood. Stallone was an investor in the theme restaurants, along with Schwarzenegger, Bruce Willis, and some other Hollywood heavyweights. Stallone was fun to interview, and always a good sport for a photo op—as he was for me.

Gérard Depardieu

I got word that I was going to interview French actor Gérard Depardieu at the hotel where he was staying, The Mark, on Madison Avenue. There was a little bonus for my chat— Depardieu told me he was the proud owner of a vineyard, Chateau de Tigne, in France, and he invited me to taste some of his wine. Apparently, however, he had not brought some extra bottles on his trip to the States, so I had to be satisfied with only a glass of his vineyard vino. I did get to pour, as you can see from this photo.

My interview was in the mid-80s, and Depardieu may have started something with celebrities, buying or becoming partners in a vineyard, from sports figures like Arnold Palmer, Mike Ditka, and Tom Seaver, to music stars. Madonna has a vineyard in Michigan called Ciccone (her real name); Sting has one in Tuscany; Lorraine Bracco in Sicily; Olivia Newton-John has a vineyard in her native Australia; and I once got a personal tour of director Francis Ford Coppola's vineyard in California's Napa Valley. During my interview with Depardieu, he said, "I love wine, because it puts me in good humor."

I'll drink to that.

Chapter 9

Working the Red Carpet

My early showbiz interviews really were the curtain-raiser to what would happen much more in the 1980s, as I gravitated to the world of entertainment. Early on, one of our veteran correspondents had dubbed me "Mr. Media," because of my celebrity interviews. In 1982 our news chief sent me out to Los Angeles to cover the Academy Awards for the first time. I didn't have to go it alone: ABC engineers were with me, including Mary Lou Grisell, who flew out from New York; and backstage it was John Price, an L.A.-based tech.

It was a heady assignment, to say the least. There I was on the red carpet talking to Oscar nominees and others who were part of what was known as "Hollywood's Big Night." Of course, I'm often asked about "those fancy Oscar parties you went to." Sadly, the answer is "There were none." After the show and Q & A with winners, I had to rush back to our L.A. studios to file reports for the morning. I would then get a couple of hours of sleep and be back at the studio at 4 a.m. to do live interviews with our ABC station's morning show hosts about the big night. But still, covering the Academy Awards was an experience I'll never forget. I did it for 25 years.

I usually had a small camera with me (no digital cameras or cell phones in the early days), and sometimes I took a few photos with the stars as they came down the red carpet. There's one photo that shows just how close I would be to the celebrities as my TV colleagues and I did quick interviews with the stars, some of whom were Oscar nominees. My colleagues covering the Academy Awards included Roger Ebert, Gene Siskel, and, from ABC, Joel Siegel and Sandy Kenyon, who was with New York's WINS, and later, WABC-TV.

Bill Diehl with Gene Siskel and Roger Ebert.

Barbara Walters

Barbara Walters's career began in 1962 on NBC's *Today Show*, with Hugh Downs. The daughter of nightclub owner Lou Walters, Barbara was surrounded by celebrities at an

early age, which has been said to account for her relaxed manner when interviewing famous people. She stayed at *Today* when Downs left and Frank McGee was hired. Although his salary was twice what she was making, when McGee died in 1974, a clause in her contract gave her the title of co-host, becoming the first woman with that title for any network news or public affairs program. Two years later Walters joined ABC News, as the first female-co-anchor of a network evening news program, working alongside Harry Reasoner. Their pairing did not produce good ratings and in 1979 she worked as co-host and producer for the ABC newsmagazine *20/20* again appearing with Hugh Downs. Walters also began producing her own *Barbara Walters Specials* and starting in 1997 she created and began co-hosting a daytime show, *The View*.

I was never intimated by Walters during our many chats about her specials. She was always very cordial but wasn't the easiest to interview when the tables were turned. Since our interviews were almost always on tape, she would sometimes ask me for a retake saying she could say it better a second time.

Remember when Katharine Hepburn told Walters that she was like an old tree and Walters asked what kind of a tree? Hepburn said, "a great oak." Walters said for years afterward, it was said that I was often asking people what kind of a tree they wanted to be, but "the only one I ever asked that question to was Hepburn." Making people cry? "Look Bill, there are certain questions that if you ask people about their childhood or if they have a parent who has died, very often tears will come to their eyes."

Asked about her father who ran the Latin Quarter in New York, Walters told me, "He did beautiful shows but he had no understanding of money. I had a sister who was borderline retarded. I always had to work. And my father lost everything when I was still in my 20s. Almost the rest of their lives I had to support them one way or another and I knew that I had to take care of my sister. When I read stories that I'm driven and must work, that was the impetus."

When I asked if Barbara Walters has a philosophy by which she lives, she said it's very simple, "this too shall pass."

In 1984, ABC Radio News moved to brand-new studios a few blocks from Lincoln Center, at 125 West End Avenue, coincidentally also a former automobile garage and dealership, as 1926 Broadway had originally been!

I was more and more concentrating on entertainment news, and was named ABC Radio's chief entertainment correspondent, and no longer doing network hourly newscasts. My program, *Bill Diehl's Spotlight*, was now offered to stations as a daily feature, and it was much easier to land some of the big stars, who often would come to our studios.

There was a publicist assigned to some of my famous-star interviews, and quotes from some of them were sent out to wire services, and they then showed up in newspapers across the country. I also began doing movie reviews, and my quotes for films showed up in newspaper ads. The first ad, however, for *Arthur 2*, got me in trouble.

As I was leaving the screening, a publicist asked me what I'd like to say about the film. I said, "A barrel of laughs. Great summer entertainment." It turned up in a newspaper ad, and my boss at ABC said I wasn't allowed to give quotes. But a few years later, when I started doing regular movie reviews on air, my quotes were everywhere, and the people at ABC were happy for the publicity—not just for me, but for the network.

Breaking news: I killed Bob Hope on the air, and he wasn't dead. It happened on June 5, 1998. My pre-recorded obituary, along with clips of some of Hope's jokes, went out on an ABC newscast after Arizona congressman Robert Stump announced on the House floor the passing of the great comedian. Stump had seen it on a wire machine in his office, but it was a "test" message. A call to Hope's

ABC NEWS ERRONEOUSLY
REPORTS BOB HOPE DEATH!!!

DRUDGE REPORT

publicist, Ward Grant, set the record straight—Hope was very much alive—but by then the damage had been done, and it quickly went up on the *Drudge Report.*

I had interviewed Bob Hope a number of times, and in one of our chats, he told me he was going to have a chat with his old friend Ronald Reagan about gun control. Hope said, "I don't see any reason why we shouldn't have gun control. It doesn't mean hunters would have their guns taken away from them; they're just registered. What's wrong with that?" The battle over gun control is still raging to this day.

SEXY LADIES
Raquel Welch

Having a photographer assigned to cover my showbiz interviews was quite a treat. Later on I always brought my own camera, and most of my interviewees were cooperative. Not so with Raquel Welch. She didn't want a photo released that she had not approved. Problem solved when her husband told her he would take a picture of us with their Polaroid camera. Rocky, as he called her, approved the photo.

Linda Gray

Age was a very gray area for *Dallas* star Linda Gray, and my interview made the syndicated *Suzy* gossip column.

Gray got into a dither when I innocently asked her (she was the mother of an 18-year-old) if it was okay for me to ask her about turning 40. "No you can't! Erase that! I'm 27, not even a day over 27. I'm ageless."

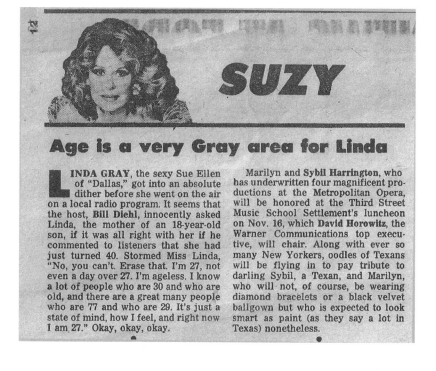

Age is a very Gray area for Linda

LINDA GRAY, the sexy Sue Ellen of "Dallas," got into an absolute dither before she went on the air on a local radio program. It seems that the host, **Bill Diehl**, innocently asked Linda, the mother of an 18-year-old son, if it was all right with her if he commented to listeners that she had just turned 40. Stormed Miss Linda, "No, you can't. Erase that. I'm 27, not even a day over 27. I'm ageless. I know a lot of people who are 30 and who are old, and there are a great many people who are 77 and who are 29. It's just a state of mind, how I feel, and right now I am 27." Okay, okay, okay.

Marilyn and **Sybil Harrington**, who has underwritten four magnificent productions at the Metropolitan Opera, will be honored at the Third Street Music School Settlement's luncheon on Nov. 16, which **David Horowitz**, the Warner Communications top executive, will chair. Along with ever so many New Yorkers, oodles of Texans will be flying in to pay tribute to darling Sybil, a Texan, and Marilyn, who will not, of course, be wearing diamond bracelets or a black velvet ballgown but who is expected to look smart as paint (as they say a lot in Texas) nonetheless.

Caroline Kennedy

My 1991 interview with Caroline Kennedy (Schlossberg) took a surprising turn, at least for me. Kennedy was joined by Ellen Alderman, for a book they had co-written, *In Our Defense, the Bill of Rights in Action.* At one point during the interview I told Kennedy that when she was married in 1986 and was on her honeymoon in Hawaii, it was reported that a member of the paparazzi had rented a room next to hers. Our interview was being taped, but at that point the door to my studio opened and her publicist said, "Bill, I don't think we want to go in this direction." Kennedy said nothing and I moved on but the interruption was strange in the midst of a discussion about the Bill of Right and First Amendment freedom of the press. Caroline Kennedy of course is now the U.S. Ambassador to Japan.

Cher

Cher, one of America's most iconic entertainers, was fun to interview. The singer, who became famous in the '70s with her husband on TV's *Sonny & Cher Comedy Hour*, also established herself as a solo artist with a string of hits. She became a movie star too, winning a Best Actress Oscar for *Moonstruck*.

In 1990, when I asked about her reputation for being outspoken and wearing revealing outfits, Cher told me, "I wasn't put on this earth to explain myself to people. You like me, you don't. You like my work, you don't. That's your prerogative, and that's fine with me."

Dolly Parton

What fun to interview Dolly Parton. Johnny Carson, gazing at her ample bosom, once said, "I'd give a year's pay to see what's under there." That was years ago of course when censors didn't let a line like that go further. But in a 1992 interview when I asked Parton about being well endowed, she blurted out, "Bill, these are my two best assets!" In a more serious vein, I asked Parton if celebrities should be giving out advice. "Well I think it's a great responsibility but there's a need for people who need help." Parton wrote a song called "Light of a Clear Blue Morning," of which she said when she was starting out trying to make it in the business, it was a kind of traveling song, traveling from one part of the country to another.

"When I wrote that song, I didn't realize it was a song of deliverance from me and a song of freedom. I've been my worst and only competition. I don't try to compete with

others. I want my songs to mean something. I love to dream, as long as God sees fit to let me be in good health. I'm not a selfish dreamer, but I'm definitely a dreamer."

Jane Fonda

Ever since *Barbarella* I have been an unabashed fan of Jane Fonda, but I also admired her for serious roles, like 1981's *On Golden Pond*—the first time and only time she worked with her father, Henry Fonda, and the first time and only time her father had worked with Katharine Hepburn. In fact, Jane Fonda said, until this film, Henry Fonda and Katharine Hepburn had never even met. In real life, Fonda said, there were times when she wasn't sure he loved her and felt he wished that she had been born a boy. "Consequently," she said, "the big scenes between us, the sort of confrontation scenes, were things that I always wanted to

say to my father and had never said. And we both knew it. It was very, very moving for both of us."

Jane Fonda became famous in the 1960s in such films as *Cat Ballou, They Shoot Horses, Don't They,* and *Barefoot in the Park,* co-starring with Robert Redford. It was in 1968 that she starred in what would become a sci-fi cult classic, *Barbarella,* directed by her first husband, Roger Vadim.

Fonda won her first Academy Award in 1971, playing a prostitute in the murder mystery *Klute.* A second Oscar came her way in 1978 for *Coming Home,* the story of a disabled Vietnam vet trying to return to civilian life.

Fonda took a lot of heat for her political activism. She was nicknamed "Hanoi Jane" when she went to North Vietnam in 1972 and was photographed sitting on a North Vietnamese anti-aircraft gun. In a 1981 interview I asked Fonda about a *Parade Magazine* cover that said, "Why is Jane Fonda Hollywood's Angry Woman?" The reason? Fonda told me, "'cuz I'm a woman. If I were a man and did exactly the same thing I do as a woman, they wouldn't call me 'Hollywood's Angry Man.' They would say I was a concerned citizen. I have found from the very beginning of my activism that the words used to describe me—*nag, nag, nag, angry woman*—so I think it's a form of sexism. I'm not angry, I'm a concerned citizen, like a lot of other people."

As for trying to shed her tag of "Hanoi Jane" because of her trip to Vietnam, Fonda said she thought she had grown since then. "If we have any sense of it at all, we try to learn from our mistakes. We mature, we try to find better ways, more productive ways, to express ourselves." Later, in a 1988 interview, Fonda apologized to all Vietnam vets and their families, saying, "I will go to my grave regretting that photo of me on that anti-aircraft gun."

Asked about getting older, Fonda said, "I worry about that, because our society is a lot less forgiving of women who get older than they are of men. But I also feel that's just the physical side of it. Inside me I feel so much happier than I did when I was younger, and as long as you refurbish and nurture your insides, your spirit and soul and mind, and you remain healthy, then it doesn't matter that you turn gray and get wrinkles." These days Jane Fonda who is heading toward 80 is still as attractive and elegant as ever. She's playing a 70-year-old, co-starring with Lily Tomlin in the Netflix series *Grace and Frankie*.

Ann-Margret

I wasn't trying to be Barbara Walters when I interviewed Ann-Margret. But when I asked her if she ever had a fling with Elvis Presley (they made several films together), she got all teary and said, "I can't talk about it, it's very personal to me." I reminded her that the British press had said that she and Elvis were actually engaged; what about that? "I'm not talking," said Ann-Margret. But she lightened up when told that it's been said that of all of Presley's leading ladies, Ann-Margret will always be No. 1. "That's sweet," she said. And I noted that as for their on-screen chemistry, especially in *Viva Las Vegas*, the word was that she was not acting. "Elvis was an American original," said Ann-Margret. "He had a profound impact on the world. He changed music."

In 2001 Ann-Margret played Miss Mona, the "ever-lovin' brothel queen" in a touring company of the musical, *Best Little Whorehouse in Texas*. Many TV stations, she said, refused to run commercials for it unless the word *whorehouse* was bleeped. A congressman wanted to ban the show's billboards, and the New York City Transit Authority banned an ad that said "Have Fun at the Whorehouse."

Lynda Carter

Lynda Carter gained her biggest fame playing TV's *Wonder Woman* in the 1970s, first on ABC and then CBS. Carter always loved to sing, even spent some time on the road with a band. She was Miss World in 1972 but then she was cast as the super-heroine. At 56 she launched a cabaret show. Feinstein's at the Regency in New York is where I saw her and she was pretty good. In my interview Carter said, "They come to hear me sing because of *Wonder Woman*. I'm not trying to avoid it, however they will also get to know me in a different way." I told her that being so well known for a role like *Wonder Woman*, can be a blessing and a curse. "That's true," she said "and I remember hearing Dustin Hoffman when he was up for an Academy Award, saying I've done

so many things, goofy, off-beat characters, yet people come up to me and say I remember you in *The Graduate*." Then she added, "I liked *Wonder Woman*, it was a great role, girls and boys liked her too."

MASTERS OF COMEDY

Mel Brooks

Mel Brooks was a hoot to talk to. "Comedy," he said, "is one of the most durable products known to man. It has more immortality in it, the diamond-hard immortality that drama will never have, because it sanitizes the world, it points a finger at social inequality and it celebrates and castigates our human eternal behavior." Asked to pick a time in history that he would want to live in, Brooks replied, "It would be the French Revolution, and I would be the King of France, and have my way with women and dwarfs and do

anything that my fantasies would allow. I would have loved it right up to when they marched me off to the guillotine. I don't think I would have liked that very much."

Carl Reiner

Carl Reiner made his mark as a comic actor with Sid Caesar in the early 1950s on television's *Your Show of Shows.* Reiner also teamed up with Mel Brooks for a funny skit—that became several comedy records—called "The 2,000-Year-Old Man." Brooks played the old man and Reiner interviewed him with lines like "What was your diet like?" "Only what God made, organic and natural, like clouds and stars." Reiner developed a TV comedy called *Head of the Family.* But the network didn't like Reiner in the starring role. It was recast in 1961 as *The Dick Van Dyke Show.*

Did Reiner think *Your Show of Shows* would become a TV classic? Reiner said, "We knew we were doing something good. With *The Dick Van Dyke Show* I knew we had something special, because it was about me. Not that I'm special, but anytime you write about yourself, you're writing about everybody."

Director Reiner's work included *Where's Papa* and *Oh, God.* He co-wrote and directed films with Steve Martin, including *Dead Men Don't Wear Plaid, The Man with Two Brains,* and *All of Me.* He played a thief and con man in *Ocean's 11* and a sequel. Reiner was the voice of a lion on an animated TV series, *Father of the Pride.* In a 1996 interview I asked him if you have to be of a certain age to be a legend. Reiner said, "I think you have to have done three important things. I've done *The Dick Van Dyke Show, Your Show of Shows,* and *The 2,000-Year-Old Man.* I've done a lot of pictures in between, but I think the thing they remember me most for are those three, so I guess that makes me a legend. Either that, or some publicist just decides, he's legendary."

One thing for sure—Carl Reiner became an American original.

George Burns

I met George Burns when he was 87 and promoting a book, *How to Live to Be 100 or More.* I asked him if *he* wanted to live to be 100. "Why not?" he said, adding, "I've got all kinds of old jokes and I've got to use them." Burns then said, "People practice on getting old. They have a tendency to fall in love with their bed. Jack Benny once told me that he 'didn't sleep last night,' and I asked him, 'How did you sleep the night before?' He said he slept great. So I told him, 'Then sleep every other night.'"

Burns made one of my ABC newscasts in a rather strange way. I had written a "news in brief" headline about who might be chosen Secretary of State. For some reason I had forgotten to insert the name as one of the favorites, and so I ad-libbed "and for Secretary of State, George Burns."

Of course it should have been George Shultz. My gaffe made Earl Wilson's Broadway column.

Jerry Lewis

Jerry Lewis and Dean Martin were one of the great comedy teams. They got together in 1946, and within six years they had created a dynamic duo, the hottest attraction in night-clubs and then on TV and in movies. In my 1982 interview with Lewis it was a given that I had to ask him about the 1956 breakup with Martin. Lewis was totally candid, telling me, "The kind of response we got was as though we had killed somebody. And I understood that, I really did. Except that what I wanted the public to understand was that we had lives that needed fixing too. But there was no time to say that, not in those days."

Was he apprehensive about going out on his own after the split with Dean? "You like breathing?" he said. "Frightened to death. First of all, I had a double whammy going. One, I provoked the split. No two ways about it. I got it on. We might have both been guilty for the motivation and so on, but I really saw to it that it got done. I felt the whole country knew that it was me, that I had destroyed something they loved, and now I'm not going to be welcome in their home. And I was prepared for whatever was going to come down. But I knew I did the right thing for me, and I wasn't thinking about the world, I was thinking about me."

And how would he describe his feelings for Dean? "I tell them, just look at my sons. Open me up and put my partner in the middle and you'll know what love is." Despite all of the anger over the breakup with Dean Martin, Lewis said, "I believe I'm a good man. I like what I've become in spite of what anyone will say, and I get stronger with the more heat I take. I will never roll over and play dead. So for those that are trying, they might as well go to someone else."

In 2009, at the Academy Awards, Jerry Lewis was honored with the Gene Hershel Humanitarian Award. Eddie Murphy, who starred in a remake of Lewis's *The Nutty Professor*, presented the award. In his acceptance speech, Lewis said, "The humility I feel is staggering, and I know it will stay with me for the rest of my life."

Bill Cosby

Bill Cosby was everybody's favorite dad—at least until allegations surfaced of sexual misconduct in which he allegedly drugged and sexually assaulted young women. Writing about him now is not easy. Here was a comedian I interviewed several times and always admired.

In a December 2001 interview, I mentioned before taping started that my daughter, Suzanne, was now a doctor,

a doctor of child psychology. Cosby was excited about that, and urged me to call her so he could say hello and congratulate her. I tried to reach her by phone but she did not get through to our studio before the interview was over and Cosby had left.

The "Cos" was there in town promoting a book called *Cosbyology: Essays and Observations from the Doctor of Comedy.* "I like to think of it as medicine," he said, "good medicine, a time to laugh." Our interview came only a couple of months after 9/11, when terrorists flew planes into New York's World Trade Center twin towers. Our interview, like others, was warm and friendly. Cosby talked about how he dropped out of high school, Germantown High in Philadelphia, and joined the Navy. "I spent three years in the tenth grade; my father said I started looking like the janitor, and he was afraid I might be arrested."

Cosby covered a fairly wide range of subjects in our studio chat. Married 37 years by then, he found it odd that married guys will say their wife is their best friend. Cosby said, "Do you love her?' I asked one guy, and he said, 'She's a gift from God.'" Cosby continued, "The personality of your wife is not the personality of a friend. I can loan a friend money, can't do that with a wife."

I asked Cosby where he was on 9/11. He said he was home in Shelburne, Massachusetts, watching C-Span. "I love C-Span; the callers, like you, are non-combative." But then came word of the 9/11 attacks and Cosby said he went to a news channel. "What had happened was like watching the *Titanic* go down, Pearl Harbor, the atomic bomb we dropped on Hiroshima."

Did he know early on in his career that he could be funny? "Yes I did—without knowing it. I studied it, listened to comics on the radio, read newspaper comic strips, and developed my own style." Did he change the face of television? I asked. "I don't think I changed the face of anything." But what about your show *Cosby*? "We decided we would have story lines that had a lot to do with family. We were not going to wiggle our heads and say 'Honey Chile, who you is and what you was.'"

On children's television Cosby created *Fat Albert and the Cosby Kids*. Toward the end of our interview I asked if he enjoyed Christmas. "I love Christmas," he said, "but I grew up poor; sometimes my parents were broke." Cosby said that comic Red Foxx told one of his favorite stories. "Foxx once said, 'We were so poor that my father went outside on Christmas Eve, fired a gun, and came back inside saying, 'Santa just committed suicide, so no worry this year about presents.'" "Sick humor," said Bill Cosby, but it said a lot about growing up poor. My admiration for Bill Cosby will never be the same; his once great reputation has been tarnished for the rest of his life. But for a time, he was one of our great actor/comedians.

George Carlin

I interviewed George Carlin, for his book, *Brain Droppings*. His thoughts on life? Carlin said, "Life is a big game. It's a circus, it's a dumb comedy parade, this whole humankind thing. It's meaningless. There's no man in the sky watching us, and we're all running around trying to buy salad shooters and sneakers with lights in them."

I told Carlin that I loved the chapter about our obsession with the past. Carlin said, "We need to remind ourselves of what's *not* going on. If it's not Bambi's anniversary or *Gone with the Wind*, then it's the Bay of Pigs." How about Elvis Presley, and those anniversaries of his death? "He seems bigger than he was in life," Carlin said, "bigger perhaps even physically."

Phyllis Diller

Phyllis Diller's professional career as a comedienne did not begin until 1955, when she was 37. She had delayed her professional aspirations when she married and raised five children. When she did launch her career, she became a pioneer in the arena of stand-up comedy for female entertainers. By 1961 she was appearing on network television, including *The Jack Paar Tonight Show*. Part of Diller's distinctive comic style was her ability to laugh at herself and those closest to her. Asked about facelifts, "I've had two of them, but if I have another one," she joked, "it will be a caesarian."

Although she was divorced when I interviewed her in 1981, Diller was still recounting tales of her fictitious husband, who, she called Fang. "I would be throwing away thousands of dollars of material if I took Fang out of my act. People love Fang, he has a wonderful image. The eternal lie-down slob."

People identified Diller by her laugh—a cross, she said, between a bull elephant's roar and a hyena's laugh. Where did that laugh come from, I asked. "It happened from nerves. I was so nervous that for the first five years I shook, I was a blur." Diller told me there were people who advised her to get rid of the laugh, but they were wrong. "You see, you have to know about advice. Advice is what you pay for, and I figured that if they knew more than I did about showbiz they would be standing in the white-hot lights. They wouldn't be sitting in their seats and then coming back and telling me what to do."

Joan Rivers

Can we talk? If Joan Rivers was still alive she'd undoubtedly have a lot to talk about with Donald Trump as America's new President. I interviewed Rivers several times including at her Carlyle Hotel suite where this photo was taken in 1981.

The last interview was for her 2010 documentary *Joan Rivers: A Piece of Work*. Rivers said, "Life sucks and you'd better enjoy it because that's a reality show. Enjoy it now while your legs are moving because you can cross the street tomorrow and you're down, lying there in bed." When I asked if she had any regrets, Rivers came up with a favorite quote, "You only regret things you didn't do. I don't regret anything I've done because at least I've done it, I've tried."

One thing Rivers did do was become the first woman to host a late night TV talk show. That was in 1986. It wasn't a success, lasting only seven months and it caused a rift between Rivers and her mentor Johnny Carson. She had been his permanent fill-in on the *Tonight Show*. But when she signed up for her own competing program, without telling Johnny first, he never spoke to her again.

Joan Rivers was a television pioneer with a career in comedy that spanned many decades until her death in 2014. In 1968 *New York Times* television critic Jack Gould called Rivers "quite possibly the most intuitively funny woman alive."

Lily Tomlin

If Phyllis Diller became one of the first big female comics, Lily Tomlin was another who was instrumental in breaking the male monopoly on humor. "Women," Tomlin told me "weren't supposed to be funny because in the past most women doing comedy had to do demeaning, self-demeaning comedy or scatter-brain comedy." Tomlin said she never dreamed of stardom growing up. "My neighbors in Detroit were a lot more interesting than Rita Hayworth or Lana Turner. I was never motivated to reach the top. I just wanted to find something that would be gratifying and I didn't care how much money I made. I was just happy making a living. I was happy in a coffee house doing a little monologue and sweeping up the floor, helping people get in and building material." How does she feel now, being on top? "Sometimes I feel different when I talk to old friends who never really got the acknowledgement that they might have gotten or probably deserved. That's the only time I feel different." I had to ask Tomlin about those wonderful characters she had created like Mrs. Beasley. "I know that I do Mrs. Beasley well because she just lives in my body. That comes from having lived it. I mean my mother, my aunts, it's in my genes. You tell me to be Mrs. Beasley and it's automatic." Tomlin said a lot of people thought she was older when she did a character like Ernestine, the telephone operator, 15 years older in fact. "I couldn't believe it that people couldn't see through that."

Asked if critics bothered her, Tomlin said, "I'm not saying I discount the critics, believe me, but if they start writing good things I'm going to run and pick up the paper, I'm just that human." When I interviewed her she had just created a new character, Tommy Valour, a Vegas headliner. "Kind of a cross between Wayne Newton and the innocence of a young Sinatra. I mean listen to me."

Carol Burnett

It was almost 50 years ago that Carol Burnett, who first became popular on *The Garry Moore Show*, began hosting her

own one-hour variety program, *The Carol Burnett Show*. It was a hit for 11 years as Burnett and her supporting players gave us so many hours of wonderful wacky skits that often featured guest stars. I interviewed Burnett several times over the years. This photo was from 1982 when Burnett was one of the stars of the movie Annie, playing Miss Hannigan, keeper of the home-for-girls. Burnett got a big kick out of being the film's villain telling me, "I enjoyed it, to be such an outrageous woman and to look horrible and get all that out of your system."

Mary Tyler Moore

Mary Tyler Moore starred in the classic 1960s sitcom *The Dick Van Dyke Show* but it was *The Mary Tyler Moore Show* in the 1970s for which she is best known. Moore played Mary Richards, a TV station producer. Ed Asner played Lou Grant, her boss. Moore once told me, "We managed to make it pretty real. We weren't afraid to have tender moments in a show that was about the business of getting laughs. And it was also the first time viewers got a chance to see what it was

like behind the show biz scene, what went into the writing of a television show."

The Dick Van Dyke Show was considered ground-breaking at the time, and Moore said, "Was it ever. It was the first time a male lead could be funny without being a buffoon." Some joked about the so-called "miracle pregnancy" on the show. "Yes, because they slept in twin beds and she wore pajamas all the time. Any time you saw these two get up in the middle of the night, she was in pajamas right up to her knees."

Moore was nominated for an Academy Award in 1980 for *Ordinary People*. It was about a mother who lost one child and resents her other son's survival. In real life, Moore has suffered her share of trauma. Her sister died of a drug overdose in 1978 and her brother died of cancer after a failed attempt at assisted suicide. In 1980, Moore's troubled son Richie shot and killed himself in what was officially ruled an accident. Moore has struggled most of her life with diabetes and in a 1995 memoir *After All*, she revealed she was a recovering alcoholic. "If nothing else," she told me, "people have communicated through the years that they have identified with me, because things that have happened to me have happened to them. I showed them that if I can get through it, they probably can too."

Ed Asner

Ed Asner won three Emmys playing Lou Grant on *The Mary Tyler Moore Show* and two more Emmys in a spin-off drama, *Lou Grant*. Asner told me those seven seasons on MTM was "like a trip to Oz. Those years went by like a tornado, except a tornado was too violent. This was like a zephyr." Why did he become an actor? Asner said, "I think acting for me was therapy. I wasn't crazy about the

person that I was and when I started acting I thought I could become somebody else that I'd like better." Ed Asner has played many roles in his career, even Santa Claus, but no doubt about it, I'll always remember him best for Lou Grant on *The Mary Tyler Moore Show*, that irascible head of the WJM newsroom.

MUSIC MEN

Luciano Pavarotti

I interviewed the opera great Luciano Pavarotti twice. The first time was in 1981, at the Metropolitan Opera. During that chat Pavarotti told me "I don't care if I die during a performance; I give all of myself. I don't see my future. I don't plan my future. I just take life day after day." As for promoting opera, such as doing a commercial for American Express, Pavarotti said, "It's a way to enlarge the audience for opera and if there are some people who don't understand this, they are dumb, dumb, dumb!"

Tony Bennett

There is no doubt that Tony Bennett is one of the greatest pop singers of our time. When Frank Sinatra once told him that *he*, Bennett, was the best singer in the business, Bennett said, "It's something I'll never forget, coming from the

master of the whole romantic era of popular singing which I consider the most sane, sensible way to perform."

He was in his 80s during this interview; he told me, "I like working. I'm one of those rare animals that feel it's healthy to keep working." Favorite singers besides Sinatra? "Bing Crosby, Ella Fitzgerald, Louis Armstrong, Peggy Lee, singers with a jazz feel, who have the art of intimate singing."

Did he ever tire of singing "I Left My Heart in San Francisco"? "Never; no matter how many times I've sung it over and over. It's not like that at all, I call it my meal ticket." The song had been gathering dust for seven years until Bennett's music director, Ralph Sharon, discovered it. Bennett told me that a bartender heard him singing it and said, "If you record it I'll buy the record." It became an international hit, and now it's an evergreen, "the greatest gift a song could ever receive. San Francisco is such a glorious city. It's really America's Paris. And the public there really appreciates that I gave them a theme song."

Did rock and roll turn his career into a tailspin, as it did for some other singers of that era? "Not for a second. I don't care who says that. It didn't because I gave the public quality music." What about his name? Bennett (born Anthony Dominick Benedetto) said, "Bob Hope named me. He said the name I was born with was too long for the marquee, so we'll have to Americanize it. So call yourself Tony Bennett. I was singing at the Paramount Theater in New York and walked onstage using the name Tony Bennett. The show went over so well, and I'm a little superstitious so I decided to go stay with that name."

As for those duets with Lady Gaga that have given a new boost to both of their careers, Bennett said, "You meet someone like Lady Gaga who has a touch of genius. She's highly intelligent and creative and knows so much about performing. She sings magnificent." How does Bennett see his success? "I look at every show as my last. I have a feel for people and want them to like me. I get a kick out of making them happy."

Besides singing Bennett loves to paint. When I arrived at his Park Avenue South apartment, his easel and a painting he was working on were in the corner. Bennett said, "I was always an amateur painter, but I did a seascape of Manhattan and I got ten thousand dollars for it. I've been doing seascapes ever since."

Tony Bennett says he never looks back. "I like living right now. This is reality for me. All the great prophets say the past is imaginary and the future's unknown, so I enjoy the moment." Did he ever see himself retiring? "I don't think about that. I love my life; I like to paint, I like to sing, and as long as I can do that, it's like stealing money."

Elvis Presley

I covered two Elvis Presley conventions in Memphis, the first in 1987, on the 10th anniversary of Presley's death. Even 10 years after his death, the fans turned out in droves. I did lots of interviews, one of them with an original member of the Jordanaires, Elvis's backup group, plus live shots on ABC newscasts. We even did a one-hour special from Graceland, *Remembering Elvis: 20 Years After*. My sister-in-law, Barbara Buscaglia, a big Elvis fan, was with me, acting as an unpaid assistant, and she was very valuable, offering plenty of helpful background information and stories about the man they called "The King."

Later, back in New York, I happened to see one of our ABC desk reports, written by editor Kevin Magee, who later became an executive at Fox News, then at MSNBC. An excerpt read, "Bill Diehl interviews a psychic who says Elvis is playing concerts *on the other side.*" Says Magee, "I wonder if there is festival seating." The desk report ends with this Thought for the Weekend: "The planets will be in alignment and Bill Diehl will be at Graceland."

Harry Belafonte

Harry Belafonte was 85 when he came to our studios, and several younger female ABC staffers were so excited to see him that they wanted a photo with him. Belafonte of course is best known for singing "The Banana Boat Song," with its signature lyric "Day-O." It was on his 1956 breakthrough album, *Calypso*, but it almost didn't make it there. Belafonte told me that when he delivered the album to RCA he was told it was four minutes short. "I had to find another song, and 'The Banana Boat' was one I had sung before, so I kinda pumped it up and made it ready for the album. And when it came out I was amazed how the world took to it." "As for Day-O," Belafonte said, "I've had priests shout it to me in the confessional!" *Calypso* became the first million selling LP album.

Belafonte, who is approaching 90 as this is written, has been a champion for social, political, and humanitarian

causes. Belafonte said that people have told him that his journey with Dr. Martin Luther King solidified their belief in nonviolence, social integration, and people coming together and caring for one another. Robert Redford, in the documentary about Belafonte *Sing Your Song,* described Belafonte as "a man whose story should be told for generations to come." As for today's young singers, some, he said, come along too quickly and pay too much attention to the gods of profit and too little attention to content. "We have a responsibility to produce music that combines culture with content." Belafonte said he loved Bruce Springsteen's album called *Wrecking Ball.* Some cuts on the album, he said, are stunning, "taking me back to Woody Guthrie, Pete Seeger, and Bob Dylan. Songs with purpose and joy that are inspiring."

Johnny Mathis

"Sports was a very big part of my upbringing, through high school and college, but music was what I was close to the most," Johnny Mathis told me. "During the week I was to make my first recording for Columbia records I had to decide whether to go to the Olympic trials as a high jumper

or go to New York to make my first recording. "At the age of 20 Mathis made two of his most popular recordings, "Wonderful, Wonderful" and "Chances Are." Mathis branched out into acting, singing the title song for the movie *A Certain Smile*. I told Mathis that his singing has been the soundtrack for many romantic evenings. "I'm flattered to be a part of so much intimacy in the world." Does he ever think about retiring? "Well, I don't think people like myself ever retire. You just stay as long as you can, and even when you can't, you try."

Barry Manilow

Singer/songwriter Barry Manilow has been on the music scene since the early 1960s. He's pretty much a household name for many people of a certain age. In our interview, Manilow talked about the importance of music. "It can tug at our emotions; it should not only make you feel good, it should also make you feel deeper." About those iconic songs he's so known for, I asked him if fans want him to

sing them at concerts. "As I've toured over the years, it gets more difficult to figure out which ones to leave out and which ones to perform. But I know they'll wanna hear 'Copacabana,' 'This One's For You,' 'Mandy,' and 'I Write the Songs,' so I'll try to please everybody." And then, looking pensive, Manilow told me, "I think that after all is said and done, what you do isn't remembered, but how you make people feel does, and that's been my whole goal—to make people feel."

Paul McCartney

I had a one-on-one with Paul McCartney just once, and it was quite a few years before he became Sir Paul and was married to Linda. When I asked McCartney about his popularity as one of The Beatles, he said, "I'm kind of amazed we did it. We were just kids." My niece Joanne took this photo, but she had accidentally changed the lens setting on my camera and this was the result, but clearly it's me and McCartney.

Andy Williams

During the 1960s Andy Williams was one of America's most popular singers and "Moon River" became his signature song. "Pure poetry," he told me in a 2009 interview. "Two drifters, off to see the world. There's such a lot of world to see. We're after the same rainbow's end, waiting, round the bend. My Huckleberry Friend, Moon River, and me." On his TV variety show Williams often sang duets with people like Julie Andrews and Tony Bennett. When Ronald Reagan was president he declared Andy Williams's voice a "national treasure." How does it feel to be called a showbiz legend I asked? "I don't like that, sort of indicates that you're elderly." Then he laughs, adding, "Which of course I am."

Neil Diamond

Neil Diamond became one of the great singer/songwriters. At first he scored success as a writer of hits for others. Remember "I'm a Believer," by the Monkees? But then as a solo artist, Diamond hit it big with songs like "Sweet Caroline," "Cherry Cherry," "Cracklin' Rosie," and "You Don't Bring Me Flowers," which was very successful when he sang it as a duet with Barbra Streisand. In 1980 he starred in a remake of the Al Jolson classic *The Jazz Singer*, which produced three top-10 singles, including "America." Diamond said he had a strong emotional connection to that song, because it was the story of his grandparents and spoke to the immigrant in all of us.

Whenever Diamond performed in concert, fans loved to hear him sing their favorites. "These songs," he told me, "are kind of like little markers along my own professional life—and to a lot of people out there, their

own lives too." Despite all of his success and fame, he did not like to be called 'the legendary Neil Diamond.' "I try not to take it too seriously, because the one that comes to mind right after 'legendary' is 'you're older, and you're finished in the business.'"

TEEN IDOLS

I interviewed many of the teen idols from the late '50s and '60s, including Frankie Avalon, Bobby Rydell (visit https://youtu.be/wUod5WM3sc0 for an interview with Bobby), Bobby Vinton, and Paul Anka. Avalon came by with Annette Funicello, who was doing reunion chats about their *Beach Blanket Bingo* films. Sadly, Funicello, who became famous as one of the Disney Mouseketeers, later developed severe multiple sclerosis. She wrote a book about her life, and even sang the original Mickey Mouse Club closing song, "M.I.C—See you real soon—K.E.Y—Why? Because we like you—M.O.U.S.E." The MS by then was so bad that she couldn't even autograph her book for me.

Paul Anka

Paul Anka was a great guest in 2011, the year he turned 70. He reminisced about his early years as a pop star and about the songs he wrote and sang, like "Diana," in 1957. Was it written about a former babysitter? I asked. "Not quite true," he said. "Our families knew each other and she would come over sometimes to babysit. But she was about four years older, and those lyrics expressed how I felt." Those lyrics include these lines: "I'm so young and you're so old . . . oh, please, stay by me, Diana." Another Anka song, "You're Having My Baby," took some lumps. Released in 1974, it appeared on some Worst Song lists, including one from *Rolling Stone*. Anka told me he felt it was a personal song written to his wife. "I could have called it 'Having Our Baby.'" One line that drew criticism was that a woman could have it "swept from her life," a euphemism for an abortion, which the Supreme Court had legalized in *Roe vs. Wade*. Years later, the song turned up in an episode

of TV's *Glee*. Anka wrote "My Way," popularized by Frank Sinatra. He and Sinatra became good friends. Sinatra, he said, hated pop songs.

How did Anka make the transition from teen idol? "I realized," he said, "that, like singers like Elvis Presley, he had to move to another level. He hit the nightclub circuit and concentrated more on his songwriting. He wrote the theme-song lyrics for the epic 1962 D-Day film *The Longest Day*. ("Many men come here as soldiers. Many men will pass this way. Many men will count the hours as they live the longest day.") Anka famously penned the opening music for the *Tonight Show Starring Johnny Carson*, officially called "Johnny's Theme."

TALK SHOW HOSTS

Phil Donahue

Phil Donahue was a television talk show pioneer. *The Phil Donahue Show*—also known as just *Donahue*—launched in 1970 in nationwide syndication, and it often focused on controversial subjects. One show focused on Holocaust naysayers. Boy, was he ahead of his time when he focused on two young men who wanted to get married. In a 1992 interview I asked Donahue about criticism that his shows were often too tabloid. Donahue said, "If it wasn't for male strippers we would not have been able to draw an audience for Nelson Mandela."

Donahue was the first TV talk show to include audience participation. "There's a word for it," he said, "It's called democracy, and I'm proud to say it was a very important part of our programs." Marlo Thomas, Donahue's actress-wife, says, "Phil was interested in the news of the day. He was the granddaddy of them all."

Phil Donahue's TV talk show ended in 1996 after a run of almost 30 years. He came out of a seven-year retirement to host a show on MSNBC, but it lasted less than a year. An internal memo leaked to the press said Donahue should be fired because of his opposition to the U.S. invasion of Iraq.

Merv Griffin

Merv Griffin went from being a big-band singer to having his own, very popular, TV talk show interviewing some of the most famous people in government, and show business, showcasing the talents of people like Woody Allen, Dick Cavett, Richard Pryor, George Carlin, Lily Tomlin, and Burt Reynolds. Griffin said he already had written his epitaph: "I will not be right back after this message."

Bob Barker, of *The Price Is Right* fame, said he knew what he wanted on his tombstone, telling me it should read, "Have your pets spayed and neutered."

Dick Clark (pictured below) was best known for hosting TV's *American Bandstand*, and *New Year's Rockin' Eve*, from Times Square. Often dubbed "the world's oldest teenager," Clark said "I'm afraid I'll carry that with me until they call me upstairs." Clark died in 2012.

Larry King

Larry King began hosting *Larry King Live* on CNN in 1985 with a wide range of guests, including athletes, actors, and politicians. King began his career in broadcasting much the way I did. And while King did not go to college, as I did, he grew up loving radio. In 1957, at age 23, he left Brooklyn for Miami. King's first job was, like mine, as a disc jockey—at WAHR in Miami. But the station manager told him that his last name, Zeiger, was too ethnic. In his office there was a newspaper with an ad for King's Wholesale Liquors. Right then the manager said, "Let's call you Larry King." Despite being awfully nervous on the air, he calmed down and learned an important lesson: Be yourself and it won't matter what the audience thinks. His first big celebrity interview was with singer Bobby Darin in 1959, when Larry was doing a morning show on Miami's WIOD—a show he did at a deli called Pumpernik's.

I met King several times over the years, including in 2009, when he was publicizing one of his books, an autobiography. "I was going to call it *What Am I Doing Here?* because I can't believe it all happened to me. But then more responsible heads said, call it *My Remarkable Journey*, which is a little more serious." Often, during my many interviews over the years, I tried to work in the question "How would you like to be remembered?" without making it sound like an interview for an obituary. King said, "I'm sure I've left a mark, but I don't think about it. I'm an agnostic. I'm not sure what's coming. I love the business I'm in, that people understood each other better through questions I asked."

Regis Philbin

Regis Philbin and I have several connections. One of them is WNEW, where I once worked. In his book *How*

Bill Diehl with Kathy Lee Gifford and Regis Philbin

Bill Diehl with Kelly Ripa and Regis Philbin

I Got This Way, Regis says that growing up in the Bronx he loved to listen to Bing Crosby records played on New York's WNEW. Regis, a decent singer himself, met Crosby when he was the announcer on the Joey Bishop TV show. I never met Crosby but over the years I got to know "Reege," as he was often dubbed, quite well. Regis was best known as a co-host on *Live with Regis and Kathie Lee*, and then *Live with Regis and Kelly*. Regis retired from *Live* in November 2011. His co-hosts had nothing but great things to say about him. Kelly Ripa said, "People feel they know him. He's like the neighbor next door, the uncle, the friend." And from Kathie Lee Gifford, "The people who make it look easy, is Regis. Don Meredith used to say 'It ain't easy making it look easy and there's something to that.'" Donald Trump was on that final show with Kelly. Trump said of Regis, "He's irreplaceable. He's a treasure." And how can we forget "Is that your final answer?" In 1999 Regis began hosting *Who Wants to Be a Millionaire*, which became a big hit on ABC. Regis was easy to be with, witty, irreverent, and a great story teller. Regis Philbin holds the Guinness World Record for the most time spent before a television camera.

A PANOPLY OF STARS

Liza Minnelli

I asked Liza Minnelli how she sees herself. "I'm a real gypsy. When I was on Broadway in 1965, I got the gypsy role because I was known as a real hard worker, and that hasn't stopped." In my 1993 interview Minnelli talked about Michael Jackson. She complained that he had been "dragged through the most incredible publicity that I have ever read. I'm ashamed of the press, the way they treat him, especially the British press. I don't think anybody deserves to be treated like that, it's appalling." How did

Minnelli view Jackson? "This is a very dear, sweet, inno-cent, child-man."

Carol Channing

Carol Channing, who is best remembered for *Hello, Dolly*, published a book, *Just Lucky I Guess*, in 2002. Asked about *what*, she said, "The thing is, it's what a comedienne calls lovemaking, and I realized, Bill, that I've been making love to an audience." What about those imitators, especially in Vegas? "I don't know where they get those weird mannerisms. In Las Vegas once there were seven men doing me at one time." Does she like being called a living legend? "No, I think I want to be called a phenomenon."

Jodie Foster

Jodie Foster was 13 when she won her first Oscar nomination, for Martin Scorsese's film *Taxi Driver*, playing a child prostitute. Many more roles followed, but in between she went to Yale, graduating with a degree in literature. Foster won an Oscar in 1988 for *The Accused*, and took an Oscar home in 1992 for *The Silence of the Lambs*. She has also produced and directed a number of films. I interviewed her several times, one of them for *The Accused*, a difficult role as Sarah, brutally raped by three men in a bar while people watched and cheered. In that interview, Foster said that in

all her roles, "I want to open people's minds to all areas of a situation. I see a little bit of myself in everything that I do. I don't think the madness of emotion is a bad thing."

Are Oscars important? "I don't think they're important. But people like them, so they *are* important. People like cartoons too." You look like an optimist. I said. But Foster shot back, "Yeah, but I can be a pessimist too. I'm the biggest pessimist in the world. I don't like being disappointed."

Susan Lucci

Susan Lucci was best known for playing Erica Kane on the ABC soap *All My Children.* Lucci was called "Daytime's Leading Lady" by *TV Guide* and the highest paid actor in daytime TV, reportedly earning over $1 million a year.

I liked her a lot, although her media image became the butt of jokes because, despite being nominated 18 times, she never won an Outstanding Best Actress Daytime Emmy. *Saturday Night Live* asked her to host a show, and in her opening, the cast and crew, and even stagehands, were seen toting Emmys of their own. I covered most of the

Daytime Emmy shows. It was embarrassing that Lucci never won but then, in 1999, on the 19th try, she "finally" won. Announcing her name, presenter Shemar Moore said, "The streak is over!" The audience gave her a big round of applause and a standing ovation.

Peter Falk

Peter Falk was best known for playing Lieutenant Columbo in the television series *Columbo*. He also appeared in numerous films, including *The Princess Bride, The Great Race, It's a Mad, Mad, Mad, Mad World, A Woman Under the Influence,* and *Murder by Death.* He was nominated for an Academy Award twice, for 1960's *Murder, Inc.* and 1961's *A Pocketful of Miracles,* and he won the Emmy Award on five occasions (four for *Columbo*) and the Golden Globe Award once.

Besides being an actor, Peter Falk was an amateur painter. Falk discovered drawing in 1971 while acting on Broadway in Neil Simon's *The Prisoner of Second Avenue.* Falk told me that one day he had some free time and was

walking on 57th Street in Manhattan and passed by the Art Students League. "On a whim I went inside, and there in a classroom was a beautiful young woman on a platform, buck naked, and I said right there, 'That's for me.'"

Because of *Columbo*, Falk was everyone's favorite rumpled TV detective and was recognized all over the world, even in Peru. "I was on vacation at Machu Picchu," he said, "and some natives there spotted me and began shouting, 'Columbo, Columbo!' How about that for recognition!"

Peter Falk painting. Source: Used with permission of Lynn Ischay / Plain Dealer Archive.

Dr. Ruth Westheimer

Dr. Ruth Westheimer hosted a show called *Sexually Speaking* in the 1980s. It ushered in a new age of frank talk about sex on radio and TV. "When I talk about sex," she told me, "it's not to shock, it's to educate. Here is something that is free, it can be delightful and delicious in a relationship." Endlessly parodied for her enthusiasm and accent, the petite

Dr. Ruth became a household name, thanks to appearances on shows like David Letterman's. German-born Dr. Ruth often reminded men, "Don't forget to wear your condoms." When I asked her in a 1992 interview about being remembered, Dr. Ruth said, "I want to be remembered as an immigrant to this country who believed in what she was doing."

Tom Hanks

Over the years, Tom Hanks has been one of the nicest and easiest stars to interview—so natural, no puffed-up sense of himself. In a 1992 interview I asked him why he wanted to be an actor. I had read that he had been told he needed

to do something to get rid of his nervous energy. Hanks said, "You wander around a lot in high school and during college years. But there wasn't anything as much fun as being in a theater building. Being on stage, great energy, we didn't have to think about anything. It just all came very naturally. I just wound up devouring knowledge, reading plays, seeing plays, seeing how it was done. I was offered a job with a repertory company. I saw no reason to stay in school. I now had this card in my pocket that said I was a professional union actor. Hey, if I'm paying union dues, I'm not going to pay college tuition as well."

So Tom Hanks is now a legitimate actor. What was his first real movie role? "It was a hack-and-slasher movie. Re- member that era when films like that came out? 'Knife-rack movies,' we called them. A girl would be washing dishes; there'd be a knife rack by the sink. And she'd go off to the living room and return to the kitchen and notice that a knife had been taken out of the knife rack." What was that first movie, Tom? "It was called *He Knows You're Alone.* It was shot on Staten Island for all of about $700,000 or something. I got paid 800 bucks." I told Hanks he had that "boy next door" look. "Yeah," he said, "but sometimes that boy next door is Ted Bundy."

Sean Connery

Sean Connery will always be special in more ways than one. Not only did he come from humble beginnings and become a worldwide film icon, he was like Tom Hanks — very easy to talk to. I interviewed Connery twice, and in one of those interviews a film crew was following him around for a feature about "a day in the life of Sean Connery." As we walked into my studio, the film crew producer said, "Mr. Connery, we didn't quite get that shot with you and Bill walking into the studio; can we do it again?" Connery looked at her and said, "Sorry, this is HIS interview; if we have time afterwards then maybe we can do a reshoot." I

thought to myself, How about that! Connery didn't give in to the film crew, and made me feel like the most important person in his view.

Of course during my chats with Connery I had to ask about James Bond. Regarding the first Bond movie he did—*Dr. No.* in 1962—Connery said, "I never thought it would be as successful as it was and I don't think anybody else really did. In some ways it's like *The Mousetrap*, the play in London, that feeds off its own momentum, and there are always new audiences coming along."

Is it true, I asked, that when Ian Fleming was casting for *Dr. No*, he was thinking of Cary Grant to play the lead? Connery said, "Yeah, but it was totally unrealistic. The picture was going to cost a million dollars—that budget wouldn't have paid for Cary Grant's airfare, so it was quite unreasonable, and Fleming realized the film would get more value from somebody who was less known." Connery felt the newer Bond films, without him, were all about the hardware, and so full of gimmicks that the character development was lost. "It's a very personal thing, but for me, I liked the intrigue more. More of the mystique of Istanbul and the train—like in *From Russia with Love*. That sort of thing is more to my taste."

Sean Connery once said he'd like to be a happy old man with a good face like Alfred Hitchcock or Picasso. When I mentioned that to him, he told me, "What I was really saying is they lived their life on their own terms, and I think it sort of shows. I think Picasso had a marvelous face; it doesn't look like somebody who, given a choice preference, would rather be happy than sad." In 1989, when Connery was almost 60, *People* Magazine voted him the sexiest man alive. How did he feel about that? "Well," he said, "there aren't many sexy dead men, are there?"

Roger Moore

Another actor who played Bond was Roger Moore. I interviewed Moore in July of 1981. Moore was then starring in his fifth James Bond 007 film, this one called *For Your Eyes Only*. Moore told me, "I'm not worried about being typecast because I am my own type, nothing else. I am fortunate enough to do a variety of other films. I do about three in between each Bond movie." Moore said playing a secret agent does not always lend itself to a terrific speaking part. "All I get to say is 'my name is Bond, James Bond.' and very little else. But the villains have wonderful, great big speeches." As a young boy Moore wanted to be a painter and he never finished high school because he was offered a job. When he felt he had learned all he could, he left to become an animated cartoonist. "I wasn't very good so they fired me. I looked around for something that paid a lot for doing very little, and I thought that was acting. I would be ungrateful if I wished to change my life," and quoted some advice from the great Noel Coward: "You must accept everything you are offered, because when you are not working, you are not an actor." Moore said he performed his own stunts in all his movies. "I'm only doubled in the love scenes!" He admitted there are certain stunts that he can't do but "I'm not going to tell you which ones they are. I think the audience would try and guess." Moore said contrary to his apparent image he does not view himself as a sex symbol and such an image embarrasses him. He has fondness for Miss Piggy, whom he met while taping a Muppet Show in London. "I spent many wonderful evenings with her."

Michael Caine

Michael Caine was born Maurice Joseph Micklewhite. Two of his best-known roles were the spy Harry Palmer in *The Ipcress File* and the womanizing character in *Alfie*. Caine has won two Oscars—the first as Best Supporting Actor in 1986 for *Hannah and Her Sisters*; the other, in 2000, for Best Actor in a Leading Role, for *The Cider House Rules*.

Are Oscars important? Caine once told me, "They're important enough to be [important] in the business that people respect you. And if you look back on who's won Oscars, with very few exceptions you would be proud to be in their company." Caine played a drunken Sherlock Holmes in 1988's *Without a Clue*. Caine said he got a kick out of playing a sort of bumbling, comedic Holmes. "It's a pleasure to do comedy, because as you get older

you even start to look funnier, and it's a great satisfaction to hear people laughing in the theater, really enjoying themselves. In a drama you don't know if they're really enjoying themselves, especially if they start going to the toilet or coughing."

Would Caine have made a good detective? "I think I could," he said, "because actors are very observant; we're looking at people—the way they move their hands, their gestures, body language. We had a very famous traitor in England, Kim Philby, who at the same time he was in MI6, was in the KGB. There was this suspicion in England and he showed up on British television in interviews, three or four years before they caught him. An American commentator asked Philby if he was or he was not a traitor, a Russian spy. I turned to my flat mate and said, 'He's lying,' and we knew he was lying. You can tell when you're an actor. It's very difficult for a salesman to sell things to an actor, except agents. We believe agents."

Has he ever done a movie just for a paycheck? Caine said he got a script for *Dirty Rotten Scoundrels*, and it was going to be shot in the South of France. "I just had to do it, canceled all my bookings, rented a house in France for three months and took my entire family with me. They had a holiday and I went to work. It was marvelous. And I remember, just before we finished shooting how great it was, and I love the French Riviera, one of the most beautiful places in the world."

Joan and Jackie Collins

I interviewed both sisters over the years.

British-born Joan Collins wrote a string of bestselling novels and lifestyle books, but she was best known for television's *Dynasty*, playing the beautiful and vengeful Alexis Carrington. Collins won a Best Actress Emmy in

Bill and Joan Collins.

Bill and Jackie Collins.

1983 for her role on that show. In a 1993 interview I asked Collins if she was anything like Alexis. Collins said that she was not the complete Alexis all the time, "although sometimes I can be if I lose my temper, but I don't have Alexis's manipulative pods."

Joan Collins loved writing "because I think all actors need a second string to their bow." On growing old, Collins said she has a favorite quote that fits her feeling too. "Do not resist getting old. Many are denied the privilege."

I interviewed Jackie Collins in 1993 when her novel *American Star* had just been published. I told Collins that her books were often dismissed by so-called "serious critics" "What is it with these critics, my books are selling off the shelves. Not bad for a school dropout." On her website Jackie Collins was described as "giving readers an unrivaled knowledge of Hollywood and the glamorous lives and loves of the rich, famous and infamous." But she told me, "Real life is stranger than fiction. I can't write real life because no one would believe it." But she added, "You will recognize some of the players. Men love it when I portray them as studs." Asked about sex in the '90s, Collins said promiscuity is lessening because of AIDS. "People must take care of themselves, that's why there is a safe sex warning at the beginning of my book."

Peter O'Toole

Peter O'Toole was most famous for his role in *Lawrence of Arabia*. But he also starred in the racy film *Caligula*, and had been quoted as slamming the film as "rubbish." But when I asked him about that, he said, "I am in no way ashamed of what I did in *Caligula*, because I fought like a tiger to make sure my character, Tiberius, wasn't besmirched."

Woody Allen

Woody Allen is without a doubt one of America's great filmmakers; his career spans more than half a century. Allen's early films included 1965's *What's New Pussycat*, for which he wrote the screenplay. His directorial debut was the following year with *What's Up, Tiger Lily*. Films like *Take the Money and Run, Bananas, Play It Again, Sam*, and 1973's *Sleeper* followed. *Everything You Always Wanted to Know About Sex but Were Afraid to Ask* and *Sleeper* made his career really take off. But his big breakthrough was my favorite Allen film, 1977's *Annie Hall*, which he directed and starred in with Diane Keaton. *Annie Hall* won four Academy Awards, including one for Best Director. One of my favorite lines? "A relationship is like a shark. It constantly has to move forward or it dies. And I think what we've got on our hands is a dead shark."

There have been so many Woody Allen movies, both comedies and dramas, including *Hannah and Her Sisters* in 1986, *Crimes and Misdemeanors, Manhattan,* and *Midnight in Paris,* his most successful film at the box office. Susan Stroman, who directed *Bullets Over Broadway,* the musical based on Allen's film of the same name, told me there's no one like him. "I think he's one of our great American writers. His use of dialogue and comedy is so wonderful." Asked once about his legacy, Allen said, "What does that mean? You think Shakespeare cared about his legacy?" Allen also said that he was tired of telling people that characters in his films aren't him. "It's fine with me that they think that; it can save me a lot of time and explaining that I don't have to do."

Mia Farrow

I interviewed Mia Farrow during the time she was embroiled in that nasty fight with Woody Allen. She had agreed to talk about her latest film (It wasn't one of Woody's), *Widow's Peak.* Just before I turned my tape recorder on, her publicist, Lois Smith, warned me, "Bill, if you mention Woody, she'll walk." But near the end of the interview I took a chance and said, "Mia, you've been going through a rough year. It hasn't been easy. How are you holding up?" Smith glared, but Mia gave me about a minute, saying, "You know, I just don't know about that. This has been my life, and I don't have the objectivity to say whether it would have been better another way—whether your life has been easier than mine or mine may be easier. I've had a good life. My children have given me immeasurable satisfaction. I'd be a fool to complain."

Julie Andrews

Julie Andrews, one of our great musical artists, on stage and screen, won the Best Actress Oscar for *Mary Poppins.* Sadly, in the late 1990s Andrews suffered a personal setback when

her vocal cords were damaged during a botched operation. When I asked her about that, she said, "It's heartbreaking, but to some extent I see the glass half full, not half empty." Andrews embarked on a new career, writing children's books with one of her daughters, Emma. Besides the Oscar, Julie Andrews has won five Golden Globes, three Grammys, and two Emmys.

Kirk Douglas
Born into poverty to Russian Jewish parents, Kirk Douglas rose to the pinnacle of Hollywood stardom with a unique persona and a very distinctive voice in countless roles. Douglas emerged as a full-fledged star in 1949's *Champion*, playing a boxer. It got him an Oscar nomination. He got an Oscar nod in 1952 for *The Bad and the Beautiful*, and

one more in 1956 for playing painter Vincent Van Gogh in *Lust for Life*. When I asked him what his favorite role was, he said it was Spartacus.

Why? "Because it was a great role, a big spectacle picture. The characters all came true." How did Douglas see himself as an actor? "I don't know. I just know that you try to play the parts you like." His son Michael Douglas told me his father was "larger than life. He ate up the screen, just burst out at you."

There were two interviews with Douglas—once in our New York ABC studio and then again at his home in Los Angeles. That last one was after Douglas had suffered a stroke, but he wanted to talk, and while it was a struggle, his mind was still quite sharp, and he talked for about 20 minutes.

Kirk Douglas never won a competitive Oscar, but in 1996 he was given an honorary Academy Award. Although he had difficulty speaking because of the stroke, Douglas came onto the stage saying, "I thank all of you for all these years."

Diana Ross

Diana Ross is, without a doubt, one of America's great music superstars. When I asked her about leaving the Supremes to launch a solo career, Ross said that "people loved the image of the three girls. We started something, and for us to part, people were disappointed and kinda sad." But, she added, "Change is important and movement in your life is important. You gotta learn, you gotta move on and grow up." Being remembered? Ross said, "I had always hoped my music would not be disposable, forgotten tomorrow. I wanted to do important things, but it's not about being remembered."

Sally Field

Sally Field was so warm and delightful to interview. She joked about being so disorganized in her life. "I get very depressed when I see perfect people. You know, women who have got it all together, and can figure out exactly where everything goes and who they are. I want to go home and shoot myself, because I am constantly confused. I can't even figure out what to wear in the morning."

Jack Lemmon and Warren Beatty

I interviewed Jack Lemmon several times, but one of the most memorable was at the Carlyle Hotel, memorable because Lemmon had not arrived yet, so I cooled my heels in the lobby along with our ABC public relations manager, who was quite a looker. Soon Lemmon walked in and apologized for being a bit late—"Out doing some shopping," he said. As we were about to head up to his suite Warren Beatty walked in. He was apparently staying at the hotel.

Jack Lemmon and Bill Diehl

Bill Diehl and Warren Beatty

Lemmon and Beatty had a brief conversation and Lemmon introduced me and our publicist to Beatty. Then it was on to Lemmon's suite for the interview with this terrific actor, whose films include *Some Like It Hot, The Apartment, Mister Roberts* (for which he won the 1955 Academy Award for Best Supporting Actor), *Days of Wine and Roses, Irma La Douce, The Odd Couple, Save the Tiger* (for which he won the 1973 Oscar for Best Actor), *The China Syndrome, Missing, Glengarry Glen Ross, Grumpy Old Men*, and its sequel.

Following the interview, I returned to our ABC studios. The phone rang. It was the ABC publicist, who said Warren Beatty had called her and wanted to take her out to dinner. She asked me for advice. I told her that Beatty was then a well-known womanizer and was undoubtedly looking to add another notch to his belt. I left it up to her to decide.

Years later she told me that she didn't accept his invitation, but confessed that it was most certainly tempting.

Joyce Randolph

Joyce Randolph played Ed Norton's wife, Trixie, on *The Honeymooners*. It was a role she never had to audition for. She had appeared in a *Honeymooners* skit with the show's creator, Jackie Gleason. A short while later Gleason said to his casting director, "Get me that serious actress who was on my show." Randolph said, "He didn't remember my name, but he knew I could play Trixie, so that week I started playing her, and it just went on and on. Although, when *The Honeymooners* began in the early 1950s, we had no idea it would become a television sensation."

Asked about being recognized, Randolph recalled that when her son came home once from summer vacation from Yale, he said, "Ma, it's so strange. People say to me, 'Is your mother really Trixie?' He hadn't thought much about it

until then, I guess." Being remembered? "Well, I guess if *The Honeymooners* is remembered, then I would be remembered too. I'm low man on the totem pole, but I'm there."

Liz Smith

Liz Smith became one of America's great gossip mavens. Her self-titled columns appeared in dozens of major newspapers in the late 1970s. She did not enjoy being dubbed "the Grande Dame of Gossip." Smith told me, "I think it's just one of those silly media things; the thing in America is, everybody wants to put you in a box." She said Donald Trump once tried to buy the newspaper that syndicated her column so he could fire her. What about her legacy? "Oh, I don't really care. I don't have any dreams of immortality. I'm not the 'godhead' of gossip."

Jack Nicholson

When I told Jack Nicholson in a 1982 interview that he might be up for an Academy Award, he said, "All honors

are suspect; it's a promotional device, a peer group award, and they do a pretty good job. I like glamour in the movie business, nothing grim about it. It's the greatest job you can get."

I'm with Nicholson. What I've done all these years covering the world of showbiz has truly been a great job. Imagine, getting paid to do something I love so much!

Stephen King

Best-selling novelist and horror master Stephen King writes from his home in Maine. In one of his rare visits to New York in 1986, I was fortunate to catch up with him when he stopped by our studios. He was promoting *Maximum Overdrive*, a new film he wrote and directed. What makes for a good horror picture? King told me, "You should be laughing so hard that you vomit all over your shoes." How would he describe the film? "It's a moron movie. If you believe trucks can run by themselves, you should seek psychiatric help. My idea of a moron movie is, check your brains at the

box office, let the movie roll over you. And when you go out, pick your brains up again, stick 'em back in your head and go home. And you don't stay up all night." King said, "When I was a teenager, we used to stay up 'til 2 a.m. after seeing *2001*, and say 'Man, did you see that black thing? And that old guy at the inn?'"

Would King rather write books or movie screenplays? "I'd rather write books. Writing movies is like skating. Everything is on the surface. Books are like swimming. Sometimes you drown, that's true, but at least you're wet all over. You're inside people's heads, you're outside people's heads . . . you can shift magically from place to place."

Does Stephen King agonize about critics of his work? "When I get really reamed, it hurts. It's like having skin taken off, and it sizzles. But I try to take it in stride and take a critical overview. Critics are not there to be consumer advocates." I told King that he once compared his writing to McDonald's food. "Yeah, a lot of it is being sold. It's very tasty, doesn't hurt anybody. I want people to have a good time. I'm not serving cordon bleu or French *nouvelle* cooking. It's moron food, but sometimes it sure does taste good."

Where does he do his writing? "At my home in Maine, where I have a study. It's better to keep the shadows in the corner when I write this kind of stuff. I crank up the rock and roll music to poison the atmosphere so no one gets too close, and I write." Does he show his writing to his wife? "I would rather be seen at my worst so I can fix things that are really bad, so it's possible to fix 'em. I would rather have someone say, 'Steve, have you ever thought about putting a blowtorch to it?' I have four novels that are just DOA, just sitting in a drawer somewhere. My idea of a book that's dead on arrival is that you can't even read it when you're really drunk and can't find anything good about it."

Would you be really unhappy when you're gone and they pull one out from your DOA file and publish it? "I'd roll over in my grave. What they've done to Hemingway I think is nasty. I don't think Hemingway ever wanted that to happen, it's a violation." How does King think HE will be remembered when he has left the planet? "Oh, probably as a hack who wrote some good books that will still be read, because horror has some amazing staying power. I want to be remembered as someone who wrote some books that are still fun to read. And for someone to say 'My God, we didn't realize this, but he was just as good as Herman Melville.'

Why does he write? "You write because you can't find anything in the library to read. I have all these fantasies and paranoid illusions, all these make-believe constructs. If I wasn't writin' 'em down, I'd be telling 'em to a shrink and paying him. This way, people pay me and nobody's trying to put me away."

Want to leave our listeners with something, Stephen King? "Well I could tell 'em we're having a pretty good time, considering we're going to die someday. Words to live by."

Shirley MacLaine

Shirley MacLaine is one of our finest actresses. But she's also a dancer, singer, activist, and author. She won an Academy Award, Best Actress in a Leading Role, for 1983's *Terms of Endearment.* In her acceptance speech, MacLaine said, "I'm gonna cry, because this show has been as long as my career. I have wondered for 26 years what this would feel like [holding the Oscar]. Thank you so much for ending the suspense." Then she added, "I'm not going to thank everybody I've ever met in my entire life, although with the way my mind has been going lately, probably everybody I've ever met in my entire life and the other life I might have had something to do with this."

In my interview with MacLaine—one of several—she said, "I'm convinced that I've lived before; there's no question in my mind. All of this is a question of perception. And everybody has their own reality and perceptions."

What about being ridiculed? I asked. "There's no way they can ridicule someone who deeply believes something like that. That would be like questioning the concept of happiness. How can you do that? No one can get into anyone else's skin. We have enough trouble in our own."

Taking risks? "I love to take risks. I love the danger of it, and I get a real kick out of the contradictions that people feel about whatever I do. I love to see human combustion. I don't like fighting, but I like different opinions that are expressed. It's sort of the highest form of democracy, so for me the future is gonna be about risks, probably going further out on a limb on every project I tackle." MacLaine said she's worried that technology could destroy us. "That should be our highest priority. What we do with the fact that we have become so technologically brilliant that we can destroy ourselves?"

Brooke Shields

I can't remember the event, but I was one of a number of reporters, and I was able to get a one-on-one with the lovely Brooke Shields. Not only that—her personal photographer took a photo of us. When I asked if I could have a copy of it, Brooke's mother, Teri, who was also her manager and agent, said, "You'll get the photo if we approve it." About a week later the photo showed up at our ABC studios.

Michael Moore
I was one of the first radio broadcasters to interview Michael Moore after his first documentary, 1989's *Roger and Me*, the film in which he confronts Roger Smith, chairman and CEO of General Motors, what Moore felt was the harm Smith did to Flint, Michigan, with his massive downsizing.

Moore kept making films, and in 2002, *Bowling for Columbine*, about the Colorado high school massacre, won the Academy Award for Best Documentary Feature. Moore used his Oscar acceptance speech to attack President George W. Bush; this generated some applause, but also a lot of boos. *Fahrenheit 9/11*, in 2004, was a critical look at Bush and the War on Terror. It became the highest-grossing documentary of all time.

Moore once told me that most politicians aren't stand-up kind of guys, as he put it, adding, "We don't have any shocks on our side anymore. You know guys who just go for it, stand up and have the courage of their convictions and go for what they believe in."

Doris Day

I've often been asked whom I would have liked to meet and interview, but didn't. Hands down it would be Doris Day.

Once, in the late '80s, after covering the Academy Awards, my wife and I took a drive up the California coast. Carmel, where Day lived, was a planned stopover. Several weeks earlier I had written to her asking for an interview while we were in Carmel. Her spokesperson sent back a polite reply saying, "Ms. Day does not do interviews anymore." But she DID talk in a 1992 PBS documentary called *Sentimental Journey*. In the opening she's on camera saying, "I'm still Doris Mary Ann Kappelhoff from Cincinnati, Ohio, and I ended up in Hollywood. And if I can do it, you can do it."

Day began as a big-band singer in 1939 and was only 23 when she sang "Sentimental Journey," in 1945, her first hit recording—the beginning of a career that took her to the top of the show business ladder. *Romance on the High Seas* was her film debut, in 1947. Betty Hutton was supposed to star, but when Hutton withdrew due to

REVEALED: THE WOMAN SAL MINEO LOVES BEST

MOVIELAND

APRIL • 25 CENTS
A MILLMAN PUBLICATION

16TH YEAR OF PUBLICATION

10 Stars Tell
WHEN A GIRL
SHOULD SAY 'YES'

*

The Secret
of Pat Boone's
Teenage Marriage

*

FULL COLOR PORTRAITS OF
JAYNE MANSFIELD
TONY FRANCIOSA
DOLORES HART
SANDRA DEE
PAT WAYNE

Doris Day

pregnancy, Day got the part. Day has said that a song she sang in the film, "It's Magic," has been one of her personal favorites.

By the 1950s, Day was one of the biggest box-office stars. She made 39 films, including *The Man Who Knew Too Much, Love Me or Leave Me, April in Paris, Midnight Lace,* and *Calamity Jane.* In 1958 she co-starred with Clark Gable in *Teacher's Pet. Pillow Talk,* in 1960, was one of three romantic comedies with Rock Hudson. The film brought Day a Best Actress Oscar nomination.

Robert Osborne, of Turner Classic Movies, told me that Day was a great singer and an underrated actress.

"She had that certain glow about her that great stars have, that can't be manufactured, that Marilyn Monroe had and Katharine Hepburn had, to name a few. There was something incandescent about her. She seemed so comfortable, always relaxed and just adorable." In 2011 Doris Day released *My Heart*, her first album in 17 years; it included eight songs never released and three written by her son Terry Melcher, who died in 2004 at 62. One of those songs was called "Happy Endings." Day says on the album that Terry wrote it for her and she insisted he sing it. "Terry was not only my son, but he was my buddy for all his life, a talented musician, producer, composer and singer."

Doris Day is not just a screen legend but a lifelong animal lover, working tirelessly for animal welfare through her nonprofit Doris Day Animal Foundation.

Chapter 10

Still in the Game

EVERYBODY NEEDS AN EDITOR

I was fortunate to have some terrific editors during my days as a newscaster at ABC. Hate to single out only a few, but among the best were Gil Longin, Ted Whitcomb, Elyse Weiner, Joan Scarangello, Betsy West, and Pam Rauscher. Pam was very particular in her editing, and I recall one instance when she was reading a script from newscaster Keeve Berman. "Keeve, where did you get this?" she said. Berman shot back, "I made it up!" Pam was not amused. Keeve had a wicked sense of humor, and it showed in that little incident.

Art Lagios was one of my first editors when our studios were at 1926 Broadway. Lagios was known to over-edit copy of news correspondents. There's the story of a Nixon speech promising that there would be "peace in our time" in Vietnam. Lagios changed it to read "peace in U.S. time." (The rule at ABC News back then was to say "U.S. troops," not "our troops.") Art later denied that ever happened.

Another example of newsroom humor at ABC was played out on a 30-foot-long "whiteboard" on a wall. On it were printed the names of cities with ABC bureaus (such as London), plus places around the world where ABC News had resident correspondents or stringers. The assignment editor, using an erasable marker, updated the board regularly. Bored one slow night, correspondent Bill Stoller started writing names on the board of fictitious stringers, aided and abetted by editor Gil Longin and several other newsroom folks. Among the fake names: "Ben Dover" in Athens. "Sue Madre" in Madrid. "Haoudi Daoudi" in Kuwait City. "Sum Dum Phoc" in Phnom Penh, Cambodia. This went on for a while until one morning when assignment editor Bob Garrity had not gotten to the board in time to erase the earlier work of the newsroom jokesters. Assignment manager Mark Richards was leading a tour of Japanese broadcasters through the newsroom. Pointing out on the whiteboard that ABC had reporters everywhere and . . . well, a scathing memo followed, barring any future foolishness. Editor Garrity probably knew who some of the culprits were but kept it to himself.

The Interns

Over the years I had many terrific interns. Two, who worked with me at the turn of the century, stand out: Phil Van and Lisa Zlotnick. I introduced Phil to Lisa and later they married. Phil, who graduated from NYU's Tisch School of the Arts, is now a leading filmmaker in California. Lisa, who sang with a big band orchestra for a few years after leaving ABC, moved into public relations. She now is head of media relations for Nintendo at its PR firm, Golin, based in Los Angeles where she and Phil live.

In an email Lisa wrote,

You carried me through my professional career to this day. You trusted me with what I considered to be a great responsibility as an intern, going to press junkets by myself, interviewing celebrities, coming back to the studio to cut the audio. You treated me with respect even though I was only 21 years old and as green as can be. A kind mentor, friend, and boss.

My interns were thrown into the craziness of movie junkets, and Lisa says she remembers several of them, like the one with Keanu Reeves, who answered every question with one-word answers. And how about Colin Farrell, who she said dropped so many F-bombs it was nearly impossible to edit the audio.

My funniest experience was the press junket for How High, *starring Method Man and Redman. The hotel room was filled with so much 'weed' smoke that I left feeling high as a kite. And I met Baz Luhrmann, director of* Moulin Rouge. *So many incredible experiences that I'll never forget.*

Lisa's husband Phil wrote this and it almost brought tears to my eyes:

To really understand what Bill was like during the two years I interned for him (2002/2003) you have to picture his office.

It was full of quarter-inch tapes, surrounding a big reel-to-reel tape machine, quite possibly the last of its kind in network radio studios. ABC had shifted to digital editing systems, but Bill was adamant about

cutting on tape. And for very good reason. He was an analog wizard; the John Henry of radio. While everyone else was typing and clicking, Bill was still cutting tape with alcohol swabs and a razor blade. This may sound overly eccentric, but he could turn out a news piece faster on his system than any of us could on a computer. It was like looking through a window into a magician's workshop.

Bill connected the future to the past. He was one of the few exceptions to digital progress. He wasn't just a reporter; he was an artist and a craftsman whose medium was an integral part of his style.

(I finally did come around however, not quite kicking and screaming, but I did learn to edit digitally on a computer screen but it took several years.)

Phil continues saying,

My experience working for Bill was pretty unique and singular and it definitely changed the course of my life. In college, I was writing for a now-defunct movie news site and the editor sent me to a press junket for a terrible slasher film. That's where I met Bill; at the same time I also met my future wife, Lisa, who was interning for him. I spoke to her first and I remember Bill cutting in and asked me point-blank if I was hitting on his intern. I told him I was not, which of course, was a lie. A few months later, he brought me on to intern for him as well. Points for bad behavior? I'm glad he saw past my eager-ness and total lack of social decorum.

Interning for Bill was overwhelming in the best way. He sent me to many press junkets where I got a chance to interview some of my favorite actors and directors. My most memorable was an hour-long one-on-one with Robert Altman, who was incredi-bly generous with his time and so articulate.

His publicist expected Bill, but I showed up instead. As I sat with Altman, mesmerized by his stories, all I kept thinking was: Did he have any idea that I was a terrified 21-year-old who had no right to be in the same room with him? To say I felt like an imposter would have been underselling it; I was entirely out of my depth. But as I watched Bill edit the audio, I realized that, as long as he had the answers he needed, he could craft a compelling Altman piece. He knew that I liked to ask a lot of questions and that was enough. This was one of the most ironic discoveries I made in the process of working for Bill: As an interviewer, I didn't need to be confident or experienced. All I needed was to be curious.

Bill sized me up and had a feeling I could do the job. And even though I wouldn't have trusted myself in many of the situations he put me in, Bill trusted me. He gave me the respect and autonomy to make creative decisions and interview some of the cinema's biggest icons. He was the first person who ever believed in me this way. And for that I'm forever grateful. I sincerely love the man and I'm glad he has been a large part of my life during such a crucial period.

There were many other interns who impressed me; I'm proud of their accomplishments, and I hope I played a part in their future. Jeff Rossen came to me right out of high school, and what an amazing young man! Within a short period of time he was editing interviews, using the old razor-blade technique (we were not using editing with computers yet) that I had taught him. There were times that I left some blood on the edit bar. Rossen went on to Syracuse University, working at a local TV station while getting his degree. After graduation it was on to a TV station in Detroit, then to WABC-TV in New York, and finally Jeff landed a top job as a network correspondent at NBC. In an email he wrote to me in June 2003, he said,

You have been a huge part of my life and whatever success I have.

That seems over the top, but I'll happily take that lovely accolade.

Intern Jessica Lagios was with me in 1997. Here's what she wrote in an email.

Working with Bill was priceless. He's brilliant and a relentless professional. He took his craft seriously, working meticulously, and yet taught me to relax and enjoy the moment when interviewing a celebrity. I reflect on my time with Bill often. Many of the celebrities who came into the studio for an interview are still on TV and in the movies. I remember—Jennifer Aniston told me she liked my outfit. Wow! I am grateful to Bill for taking me under his wing and offering me the opportunity to make many memories that I will always cherish.

Another intern, Emily Smolar, became a top producer at two TV stations in New York City, WNBC and WCBS. She's now a senior producer for *On the Case with Paula Zahn.* My wife and I went to her wedding. Emily was with me during the summer of 1998 and has fond memories. Here's what she wrote in an email:

> *I was sent to one of those press junkets in which actor Johnny Depp was being interviewed. Depp spent the entire time drawing a picture of an elephant's ass. Don't know why, but he left it on the table. Bill told me I should have taken it. I should have listened.*

> *I recall the time Bill had two events scheduled at the same time and handed me a tape recorder and told me to interview actor Matthew Perry. "Go by myself?" And you said, "Well you want to be a reporter, right? So go report."*

Smolar remembers a private interview at Planet Hollywood with George Clooney.

> *I had such a crush on him and told him all about how I was going to Syracuse University for broadcast*

journalism. We then got into a discussion about his dad and he agreed to take a photo with me. Still framed in my home. There were so many wonderful memories, I had an amazing summer.

My wife and I also went to the wedding of another intern, Jessica Stone. Stone, who was going to NYU in 1998, had to keep a daily log of her internship at ABC. She shared it with me years later, and it was not only enlightening but funny too. Jessica writes,

My first week at ABC News Radio has been both exhausting and exciting.

That turned out to be quite an understatement.

Diehl is nothing but charming

she writes in her log.

Debonair and a complete gentleman, he is a Clark Gable for the 90s.

Hey, I'm not bad-looking but me and Clark Gable? Wow! Jessica already had experience doing digital editing at a classical music station where she worked in Miami, and thanks to her I slowly abandoned my old ways and learned that digital was the way to go. Jessica got a big kick out of her internship.

I have never known anyone who receives as much mail as Bill Diehl. He gets so many magazines that he would never get through them all if he read magazines for a living. And then there's the endless flow of electronic press kits and screening invitations and an assortment of promotion materials, stuffed animals, posters, clocks, you name it.

While some of my interviews were at hotels, usually with half a dozen other reporters questioning an actor or actress about their latest film, it was better to have a one-on-one chat in our ABC studios. Like the one with actress Jane Seymour, star of *Dr. Quinn, Medicine Woman*. Jessica said Seymour arrived with an entourage and two giant bottles of champagne, since she had been commissioned by Korbel to design a bottle. Says Jessica:

> *The most amazing thing about this woman is that she had twins at the age of 45. I still can't get over that one.*

Just how funny is Jessica? Well, on her last day as my intern she joined me at Tavern on the Green (no longer called that) for a party celebrating Charlie Gibson's last day on *Good Morning America*. (Charlie later became the anchor of ABC's *World News Tonight*.) Jessica said,

> *I don't think I've ever had better cinnamon French toast.*

How's that for an ABC memory?

In the fall of 2007, I was given a retirement party, and I thought that was the end of my broadcast career at ABC News Radio. Not so. Early in the following year, I was called back to do some features for our ABC magazine program, *Perspective*, and advance obituaries. When Robin Williams died suddenly, I had already done his obituary. So too with Joan Rivers, and the list goes on and on.

And I've got a terrific file of tapes of stars I've interviewed over the years with wonderful anecdotes about their careers. (Nuggets of those interviews make up this book.) I've also had the pleasure of doing features on Broadway shows, interviewing people like Patti LuPone, Jake Gyllenhaal, and Bernadette Peters.

(There's a YouTube of that interview at: https://www.outube.com/ watch?v=ohwMv2PKs8A&feature=youtu.be.)

One of our ABC staffers jokes that when I arrive at our studios, "Look out, here comes the Prince of Darkness." Nothing dark about Broadway, it's "The Great White Way" . . . full of life and with great artists to interview.

I've received personal thank-you notes from some of the stars I interviewed over the years, but a note that wasn't from a star is one I really cherish. It was written by one of our ABC Radio directors on New Year's Eve, 1982. His name was Bill Gately, who passed away many years ago.

I have a copy of it. In it, Gately said he

didn't want the sun to set on '82 before telling you what a wonderful opportunity working with you on your Bill Diehl's Spotlight *show has been for me. You are a rare professional with great gifts and a wonderful sense of what is meaningful of the passing parade. Your contributions of work, time, effort, insight, and the large dollops of those special graces you have as an interviewer made the show a real gem and unquestionably the best thing the network has had to offer for some time. Now, we can lament the vicissitudes of the business or prepare for the re-emergence of sense and sensibility . . . I prefer the latter.*

That was written long ago, and while Gately is gone, reading it again now brings tears to my eyes.

When my alma mater, Ithaca College, honored me with a Professional Achievement Award in May of 2008, it prompted some wonderful accolades from friends and broadcasting colleagues. While I have interviewed many of the rich and famous, I have never thought of myself as a celebrity, but my dear friend Holly Faber, whom I first met through my wife, Lorry, in the late '60s, said, in an email congratulating me on the college honor,

> *Bill Diehl has always been my personal celebrity. When I told friends about Bill, many—mostly women—would say, 'You actually know him?'*

That was when I was working at WNEW as a newscaster. Holly wrote,

> *Later in his career at ABC he was the 'movie guy,' and I would see a blurb he had written for a film that showed up in an ad on TV or in a newspaper. I have never known anyone in my life who gets so happily excited over the little things in life.*

> *The award he is receiving will be one of the BIG things in his life, and he deserves it.*

Holly knows how to make a guy feel great and humble at the same time.

> *Now I can brag about not just knowing this wonderful man, but actually having 'touched' him. And now he has a special award for his life's work.*

*Of course, you understand, his career was never
work, it was his passion.*

Holly is right, my career has been my passion. Call it
one great ride. I liken it to what Robin Leach, who was host
of *Lifestyles of the Rich and Famous*, once told me: "I see
myself as a butler invited to take tea in the drawing room
each time I'm with a celebrity. It's a job that allows me to
combine the best of both worlds and bring the stars to my
audience." Nice work if you can get it, and I was fortunate
to be among those who got it.

Why did I decide to write a book like this? My one-
time WNEW colleague, Gene Klavan, probably put it best
in *We Die At Dawn*, the often funny story of the madcap
morning-show team Klavan and Finch. Klavan wrote in the
introduction,

> *If you never write a book, there is a good possibility
> that no one will find out the truth about you. But if
> you do not write a book, there is also the possibility
> that no one will ever find out about you at all.*

So here it is, *Stay Tuned! My Life Behind the Mic*, a
great ride that isn't as exciting as it once was, but I'm still in
the game, and it doesn't get any better than that.